The
Fourfold Gospel

The
Fourfold Gospel

A Theological Reading
of the New Testament Portraits of Jesus

Francis Watson

Baker Academic

a division of Baker Publishing Group
Grand Rapids, Michigan

Published by Baker Academic
a division of Baker Publishing Group
P.O. Box 6287, Grand Rapids, MI 49516-6287
www.bakeracademic.com

Printed in the United States of America

Library of Congress Cataloging-in-Publication Data
Names: Watson, Francis, 1956–
Title: The fourfold gospel : a theological reading of the New Testament portraits of Jesus / Francis Watson.
Description: Grand Rapids, MI : Baker Academic, 2016. | Includes bibliographical references and index.
Identifiers: LCCN 2015037207 | ISBN 9780801095450 (cloth)
Subjects: LCSH: Bible. Gospels—Criticism, interpretation, etc. | Bible. Gospels—Hermeneutics. | Bible. Gospels—Theology. | Jesus Christ.
Classification: LCC BS2555.52 .W378 2016 | DDC 226/.06—dc23 LC record available at
http://lccn.loc.gov/2015037207

16 17 18 19 20 21 22   7 6 5 4 3 2 1

Contents

Preface

A "theological" reading of the canonical gospels is one that addresses questions they pose that relate to core concerns of Christian faith. Not all gospel interpretation is theological in this sense, and with good reason. The texts raise many questions that are tangential to Christian faith yet still significant in themselves. Nor is theological interpretation just one thing. It may be practiced in many different ways, of which renouncing the tools of critical scholarship for fear of secular contamination is perhaps the least promising.

The present book takes its cue from the fact that the four gospels are also a fourfold gospel. Each text is as it is only in relation to the others. The gospel texts retain their distinctiveness, yet they are coordinated with one another and do not exist outside that coordination. The plurality is a unity and the unity remains a plurality; one can therefore speak both of "four gospels" and of a singular "gospel according to . . ." in four different versions. None of the individual evangelists seem to have envisaged any such arrangement; indeed, only one of them (Mark) even uses the word "gospel" with any real enthusiasm. The fourfold gospel is the work not so much of the evangelists as of their early readers. It is the outcome of a process of gospel *reception*, and—since reception creatively reshapes what is received—it is also an ongoing work of gospel *production*. In that work a number of well-known figures in the early church played their parts; the names of Irenaeus, Origen, Eusebius, and Jerome will feature prominently in the pages that follow. But the work of reception was also carried forward by anonymous communities and individuals who read, prayed, lived, and cared about these books and so ensured that they continued in circulation and were available to meet new needs in new contexts. The shaping of the four texts occurred not only in their initial selection and coordination but also in the provision of authorial identities and biographies, in the development of a gospel symbolism, and in the scholarly analysis and interpretation of gospel similarities and differences. By these and other means, the early church *made sense* of its own core texts, in which the one story is told and retold in four different ways.

That is the framework in which this book offers its readings of gospel beginnings and endings. In an earlier and larger work entitled *Gospel Writing*, I developed a related argument in a form that remained accountable to the modern tradition of gospel scholarship even while criticizing its limitations. The canonical perspective of that book focused on excluded as well as included texts, highlighting the new situation created by an increasingly sharp canonical boundary. The present attempt at a theological reading focuses throughout on the texts within that boundary and on the theological questions they put to their interpreter, both individually and in their relations to one another. My main dialogue partners are often ancient authors rather than modern ones—not because I believe in "the superiority of precritical exegesis" but because the nature of this particular exercise seems to require it.

In the opening prolegomena, I attempt to show how the fourfold gospel came into existence—a second-century process with first-century roots. This is ground I have already covered in detail in *Gospel Writing*, and it is no more than prolegomena here because the main body of the book is concerned not with the origins of the fourfold gospel but with its form and significance. The four chapters of part 1 are devoted to the individual gospels, and their basic premise is the patristic assumption that a gospel's unique character comes most clearly to expression at its beginning. These chapters focus on the different gospel beginnings in order to characterize the gospels' distinct theological perspectives on the one they all confess as the Christ, the Son of God. The early church represented this difference of perspective by drawing on the symbolic resources of the books of Ezekiel and Revelation, and the symbolism of the four living creatures around the divine throne—the human, the lion, the calf, and the eagle—remains illuminating. These plural perspectives are not only different but also complementary; that, at least, is how they are intended to be read, and it is how they are read here. This complementarity is to be found on the theological rather than the historical plane, for the evangelists are more concerned to bring out the fundamental significance of Jesus' life than to provide precise information about factual detail. The gospels are portraits, not entries in a biographical dictionary.

The two central chapters of part 2 (chaps. 6 and 7) focus on gospel endings, and they present readings of episodes from the combined passion narratives—the triumphal entry, Gethsemane, the crucifixion, the empty tomb—in which the same story is told and retold by all four evangelists. The fourfold gospel testimony to these events is analyzed with the help of the so-called canon tables devised by Eusebius of Caesarea in the fourth century, which not only installed an effective cross-referencing system within premodern gospel books but also classified the different ways in which gospels relate to one another. Eusebius's canon tables remain one of the most impressive achievements of early Christian scholarship, although in recent times they have been little appreciated and poorly understood. A preliminary chapter (chap. 5) is therefore devoted to Eusebius's system, which, by displaying the ties that bind the gospels together, created a rationale for including the four separate gospels within the covers of a single volume. That is how the fourfold gospel established itself as a fourfold gospel *book*.

The gospel texts converge at their endings, but the question remains as to how these texts converge on the truth itself—the truth

about Jesus, which, from a Christian standpoint, also entails definitive truth about God, the world, and human existence in the world
and before God. The question of truth is everywhere implicit, even
when the discussion seems focused only on texts, but it becomes
explicit when—in the ancient world, as today—the gospel is said to
be fundamentally *untrue* and, as such, detrimental to human well-
being. In the final chapter of this book (chap. 8), these claims provide
an occasion for historically informed theological reflections on the
nature of gospel truth.

I should emphasize that this book offers no more than a *reading*
of the fourfold gospel. It does not seek to be prescriptive. There is no
claim to the effect that Matthew's opening genealogy is the one and
only key to understanding his gospel, or that future gospel scholarship should base itself on Eusebius's canon tables. Such claims would
be unwarranted and indeed absurd. The basic observation that the
fourfold gospel exists as a singular entity in its own right might lead
in any number of different directions.

I must express my thanks to Matthew Crawford, my outstanding
postdoctoral research assistant, for his many exceptional contribu-
tions to our joint research project, "The Fourfold Gospel and Its
Rivals," under whose auspices this book has been written, and also
to the UK Arts and Humanities Research Council for funding it,
and him. In the early summer of 2014, during a period of research
leave at the Free University, Amsterdam, I benefited greatly from the
comments of four sharp-eyed and articulate undergraduate readers
with whom I met regularly to discuss drafts of the first four chapters:
Ruben van de Belt, Martine van der Herberg, André Poortman, and
Mirjam Verschoof. My warmest thanks to them and to my always-
genial host, Bert Jan Lietaert Peerbolte, who did so much to make
my stay in Amsterdam memorable. Drafts of "The Making of a
Fourfold Gospel" were presented to graduate seminars in Amsterdam,
Cambridge, Durham, and St. Andrews, and in each case significant

improvements resulted. My thanks to all who participated in these events.

In September 2014 I was privileged to deliver a series of five lectures based on the first half of this book at Trinity Theological College, Singapore. It was a remarkable experience to speak about the gospels in an Asian context where Christianity is still a relatively new phenomenon and where its rapid expansion recalls the church of the second and third centuries and contrasts with the situation in the West. I would like to thank my former student Leonard Wee, Principal Nguei Foong Nghian, and the many other faculty, students, and friends of the college who showed such extraordinary kindness and hospitality at that time. Taiwan and Charles Leung deserve a special mention here. Introducing a class of first-year students to the use of a gospel synopsis and the study of gospel parallels was a particularly memorable experience.

In writing this book I have often found myself returning to themes addressed in PhD theses I supervised during my time at the University of Aberdeen from 1999 to 2007. Thanks are due in particular to Joel Kennedy, Suresh Vemulapalli, Richard Cornell, Tom Holsinger Friesen, David Nienhuis, and Jake Andrews for many instructive conversations on (respectively) the Matthean genealogy, the synoptic "way of the Lord" motif, the Gospel of John in patristic christological debates, and Irenaeus, Eusebius, and Augustine.

The book is dedicated to my parents, with gratitude and affection, in the hope that it meets their long-standing request for a shorter book accessible to nonspecialist readers.

Francis Watson
Durham, England
March 19, 2015

Abbreviations

ANF	*Ante-Nicene Fathers*
CCSL	Corpus Christianorum: Series Latina. Turnhout: Brepols, 1953–.
CD	Karl Barth, *Church Dogmatics*
CSEL	Corpus Scriptorum Ecclesiasticorum Latinorum
FC	Fathers of the Church
GCS	Die griechischen christlichen Schriftsteller der ersten Jahrhunderte
ICC	International Critical Commentary
KEK	Kritisch-exegetischer Kommentar über das Neue Testament (Meyer-Kommentar)
LCL	Loeb Classical Library
LW	*Luther's Works*
LXX	Septuagint
NA[28]	Nestle-Aland, *Novum Testamentum Graece*. 28th ed. Stuttgart: Deutsche Bibelgesellschaft, 2012.
NKZ	*Neue kirchliche Zeitschrift*
NPNF[1]	*Nicene and Post-Nicene Fathers*, Series 1
NPNF[2]	*Nicene and Post-Nicene Fathers*, Series 2
NTS	*New Testament Studies*
ThTo	*Theology Today*
WA	*Weimarer Ausgabe (D. Martin Luthers Werke: kritische Gesamtausgabe)*
WA DB	*Weimarer Ausgabe, Deutsche Bibel*
ZNW	*Zeitschrift für die neutestamentliche Wissenschaft und die Kunde der älteren Kirche*

Prolegomena: The Making of a Fourfold Gospel

How many gospels are there? What are the names of the evangelists? It is hard to think of any more elementary items of biblical knowledge. Even at a time of declining biblical literacy, there are still many—of different ages and backgrounds, with or without links to churches—who could answer such questions with confidence. There are four gospels. The evangelists' names are Matthew, Mark, Luke, and John.

These are, of course, the right answers. Or are they? Might they be, if not wrong, at least misleading? These answers need some refining. There are four gospels *in the New Testament*, although other gospels or gospel-like texts were in circulation in the early church. It is *tradition* that names the canonical evangelists as Matthew, Mark, Luke, and John and places their texts in what is supposed to be chronological order. The texts themselves are anonymous, and their authors or editors show little inclination to make their identities known.

If the answers need refining, so too do the questions, with their taken-for-granted references to "gospels" and "evangelists," or gospel writers. The texts are universally known as "gospels," but this plural term may not be appropriate. One of them, Mark, refers to

1

itself as "the Gospel of Jesus Christ,"[1] which seems not to leave room for further gospels. In two of the others, Luke and John, the term is never used at all. The singular "gospel" originally referred to the Christian message—good news delivered in person, not in writing. The apostle Paul once pronounced a double anathema on anyone (even an angel) who tried to supplement the one true gospel with another.[2] What would Paul have made of the suggestion that there are, or should be, four gospels?

It seems that our initial naive questions and answers must be reformulated. How should we view the relationship between the four canonical gospels and gospel literature outside the New Testament? Within the New Testament, are we dealing with four distinct texts or with a single text in different versions? How did these texts or versions become associated with the term "gospel" and with named evangelists? Why are *these* four texts collected together in preference to other texts or formats? Answering these questions will provide us with an account of how the four-gospel collection was constructed. This fourfold gospel did not just happen. It did not assemble itself automatically when the Fourth Evangelist laid down his pen. It is a collective work fashioned by the evangelists' early readers.

More succinctly put, our preliminary questions about gospels and gospel writers are these: (1) More than four? (2) Fewer than four? (3) Why "gospel"? (4) Why the evangelists' names? (5) Why these four?

More Than Four?

The four-gospel collection is the foundation stone of the New Testament collection, but that does not mean that only four gospels were written. Some of the additional gospels have always been well known, appreciated by some though criticized by others. These are conventionally placed in the category of "apocryphal" gospels, and they are typically expansions of the beginnings or endings of the

1. Mark 1:1.
2. Gal. 1:8–9.

canonical gospel narratives. The *Protevangelium of James* relates the birth and upbringing of Mary as the prelude to a fuller account of the circumstances of Jesus' birth, elaborating material drawn from Matthew and Luke. The *Infancy Gospel of Thomas* contains entertaining stories about the child Jesus' not-always-benevolent use of his magical powers. The *Gospel of Nicodemus* offers the reader further information about Jesus' trial before Pilate, his death, his descent into hell, and his enemies' reaction to his resurrection. The label "apocryphal" implies that these texts are essentially different from the canonical gospels, that they were written considerably later, and that they lack credibility and authority. Presumably those who used these texts thought more highly of them than that.

More significant questions arise from the many papyrus fragments of Greek gospel books recovered from the sands of Egypt since the late nineteenth century. Most of these fragments are from volumes containing a single gospel, and the figures for each gospel can give a rough indication as to popularity and influence over a period stretching from the second century to the seventh. The two gospels attributed to apostles are far ahead of the others, with (at the last count) twenty-six copies of John attested and twenty-two of Matthew. Luke comes in third place with eight copies, but Mark (a single copy) is overtaken by the noncanonical *Gospel of Thomas* (three copies), the *Gospel of Peter* (three), and the *Gospel of Mary* (two).[3] Other fragments are from unknown gospels—"unknown" in the sense that no reference to their supposed authors has survived. Of these, the most important is the *Egerton Gospel*, named after the bequest from which the British Museum acquired its papyrus remains in 1934. If the figures are restricted to papyri dated to the second and third centuries, the proportions are about the same: John, fifteen copies; Matthew, nine; Luke, four; *Thomas*, three; *Mary*, two; *Peter*, two; *Egerton*, one; and Mark, zero. Even in later centuries, copies of

3. The figures for the canonical texts are drawn from the listings of New Testament papyri in NA[28], 792–99. On the use of the codex format in these papyri, see esp. L. Hurtado, *Earliest Christian Artifacts*, 43–93.

Peter, *Thomas*, and *Mary* continued to be produced in Greek or in Coptic translation.[4] On the basis of these figures, owners of gospel texts were as likely to possess a noncanonical gospel as a copy of Luke or Mark.

To use all available gospel texts was not necessarily to cast one-self in the role of a rebel or a heretic. This is clear from the work of Clement of Alexandria, writing in the late second and early third centuries. Clement's logic seems to be as follows.[5] Sayings of Jesus may appear in gospel texts outside the canonical four and yet give every appearance of authenticity. The canonical texts themselves make no claim to completeness; on the contrary, "Jesus did many other signs before his disciples that are not written in this book."[6] If other books contain authentic tradition about what Jesus did or said, then the literary context that preserved it is of secondary importance. It hardly matters whether it was Matthew or Thomas who wrote down a saying of Jesus; the saying and the speaker are more important than the scribe. To an Egyptian Christian of the third or the sixth century, the answer to the question "How many gospels?" might not have been straightforward. He or she would be aware that just four gospels were authorized for reading in church, and yet be convinced that authentic and valuable gospel literature was to be found beyond the church's limit.

That was also the view of Christians in Rhossus, a coastal town in Roman Cilicia located close to the modern border between Turkey and Syria. At some point around the beginning of the third century, Christians there petitioned Bishop Serapion of nearby Antioch for permission to use the noncanonical *Gospel of Peter* in their public worship. (A passion-and-resurrection narrative from this text was discovered in 1886; other early evidence seems to confirm that it was

4. For details of manuscript evidence for the noncanonical texts, see T. J. Kraus and T. Nicklas, *Das Petrusevangelium*, 25–31, 55–63; S. Gathercole, *Gospel of Thomas*, 3–13; C. Tuckett, *Gospel of Mary*, 5–10; T. J. Kraus, M. J. Kruger, and T. Nicklas, *Gospel Fragments*, 11–22 (*Egerton*).

5. For full discussion, see F. Watson, *Gospel Writing*, 418–36.

6. John 20:30; cf. 21:25.

a full-length gospel of similar scope to Matthew in which "Peter" speaks in the first person singular.)[7] Serapion, bishop of one of the major sees of the eastern Mediterranean and a determined opponent of heresy, had not read this text. Yet he was persuaded by the petitioners' arguments and duly gave them permission to use it. A little later, having become better acquainted with the *Gospel of Peter*, he wrote to the Rhossian Christians in some embarrassment, listing passages he now believed to have been added by heretics. Yet he does not deny the basic soundness of the Petrine gospel. If heretical additions are listed, the appropriate response would simply be to delete them or to make new copies that omit them—not to give up on this gospel as a whole. At this time there was still nothing inherently wrongheaded about the Rhossian adoption of a further gospel, even for an impeccably orthodox bishop. Nevertheless, the request for permission to use it also implies an established usage of other texts. We may assume (though we cannot be sure) that no one ever wrote to Serapion for permission to use Matthew, Mark, Luke, or John.

If the New Testament contains four gospels, that does not mean that only four gospels were written. It means that four gospels were selected from a wider range of gospel literature to serve as a basis for the church's preaching, teaching, and worship. The four-gospel collection is the work not just of individual evangelists but of the church.[8]

Fewer Than Four?

The texts we know as "Matthew," "Mark," and "Luke" have their own distinct identities. Yet Matthew incorporates most of the contents of Mark into his own more comprehensive framework. The same is true of Luke, who also shares much of the material that Matthew adds to

7. The relevant texts are collected in Kraus and Nicklas, *Das Petrusevangelium*. An excerpt from Serapion's letter to the church at Rhossus is preserved in Eusebius, *Church History* 6.12.1–6.

8. Thus, from a purely historical point of view, the gospels "are inseparable from the space they have inhabited, and continue to inhabit, as the canonical Scripture of the Christian church" (M. Bockmuehl, *Seeing the Word*, 77).

Mark, probably deriving it from Matthew himself.[9] Mark's narrative spans the events from Jesus' baptism and temptation through his Galilean ministry, his transfiguration, and his journey to Jerusalem to the drama of Good Friday and Easter morning. Along the way there are healings, exorcisms and other miraculous events, parables and instruction for the crowds or disciples, and debates with opponents in both Galilee and Jerusalem. Matthew, writing later, retains this basic framework but supplements it, inserting major new blocks of material at various points in the Markan outline. This evangelist wants to provide a more comprehensive account than his predecessor. He may perhaps have expected his text to be used alongside Mark's, a second gospel to complement the first. More likely he expects to *replace* Mark. His is not an independent work with himself as sole author. Matthew is not only an author; he is also an editor who takes upon himself the task of preparing an enlarged and improved second edition of the earlier gospel text. So the questions arise: Do we have here two gospels, or two editions of a single gospel? Does Luke then add a third edition? Are the evangelists more like individual authors or anonymous editors?

Mark's gospel begins with the ministry of John the Baptist, about whom a surprising amount of information is compressed into a few verses. We read of the prophetic foretelling of his ministry, his call to repentance and baptism, even his unusual clothing and diet. Jesus is introduced with no preparation at all: "In those days Jesus came from Nazareth of Galilee and was baptized by John in the Jordan."[10] Immediately the heavens open, the dove descends, and the divine voice acknowledges Jesus as "my beloved Son."[11] It is all very sudden; no explanation is given as to why this particular candidate for baptism is singled out like this. So Matthew supplies us with the background and context that make sense of the event that launches Jesus' ministry. A genealogy is provided, and a miraculous conception signals a unique

9. As argued persuasively by M. Goodacre, *Case against Q.*
10. Mark 1:9.
11. Mark 1:10–11.

divine involvement in this particular human life from its very beginning. Even the fact, noted by Mark, that Jesus was "from Nazareth of Galilee" is not an accident. Matthew devotes much of his second chapter to showing how a Messiah born in Bethlehem nevertheless grew up in Nazareth, as foretold in prophetic scriptures.

Mark's abrupt beginning is matched by an equally abrupt ending. Women disciples of Jesus visit his tomb early on Easter morning but flee in terror when they find it occupied not by Jesus' corpse but by a mysterious young man in white who announces his resurrection.[12] One second-century reader found this conclusion so unsatisfactory that he added a series of postresurrection appearances to Mary Magdalene, two disciples on the road, and the Eleven.[13] The author of this "Longer Ending" was not the only early reader to worry about Mark's inconclusive conclusion. It had already been thoroughly rewritten by Matthew, who makes the young man in white unambiguously an angel and adds a guard before telling how Jesus appeared to the women on their way back from the tomb and to the eleven male disciples on a Galilean mountaintop.[14]

So the gospel narrative as conceived by Mark is provided with a new beginning and a new ending, and there are further interventions along the way. After the Markan Jesus calls his first four disciples, he enters the Capernaum synagogue and impresses the congregation with his teaching—"for he taught them as one who had authority and not as the scribes."[15] Mark tells us nothing here about the content of Jesus' teaching, preferring to focus instead on a dramatic exorcism performed on the same occasion. Like Mark, Matthew tells of the call of the first disciples and reports the favorable audience reaction to Jesus' authoritative teaching.[16] In both cases the wording is unusually similar. Yet in Matthew the scene of the teaching is shifted from a synagogue to a mountaintop, and the exorcism story is replaced by

12. Mark 16:1–8.
13. Mark 16:9–20.
14. Matt. 28:1–20.
15. Mark 1:22.
16. Matt. 4:18–22; 7:28–29.

an elaborate and artfully structured presentation of the authoritative teaching itself, the so-called Sermon on the Mount.[17]

Matthew's editorial procedure is to add blocks of new material to the beginning and ending of Mark and at several points in between. Luke's editing of Mark is broadly similar. Following the sequence of Mark's narrative just as Matthew does, he too adds a birth story and a genealogy to the beginning and postresurrection appearance stories to the ending. He too inserts larger or smaller blocks of additional material—teaching or narrative or a combination of the two. At each point of similarity with Matthew, a contrast may also be noted. For Matthew, Joseph is the central figure of the birth stories; for Luke, it is Mary. Matthew traces Jesus' descent from Abraham and David through Solomon and the kings of Judah, while Luke proceeds in the opposite direction through another son of David back beyond Abraham to Adam.[18] Matthew sets the great Sermon on a mountain, while Luke's reduced version is preached on a plain.[19] For Matthew, the disciples' meeting with the risen Lord takes place in Galilee; for Luke, it occurs in Jerusalem.[20] The similarities and contrasts can hardly be coincidental. Although many scholars still think otherwise, it is difficult to believe that Luke writes without knowledge of Matthew.[21] Does he seek to complement Matthew, or does he regard Matthew as a rival? In his preface he contrasts predecessors who have "attempted" to write a faithful account with his own work, which (unlike theirs, it seems) is carefully and thoroughly researched.[22] Here at last is the book that better-educated Christians have awaited so long—a reliable and accurate account of the life and ministry of Jesus!

Have Matthew and Luke produced new editions of older material, perhaps even in competition with each other? Does either of them envisage any future for Mark as an independent work? Celsus, an

---

17. Matt. 5:1–7:27.
18. Luke 3:23–38.
19. Matt. 5:1; Luke 6:17.
20. Matt. 28:16; Luke 24:33–36.
21. See F. Watson, *Gospel Writing*, 117–55.
22. Luke 1:1–4.

early critic of Christianity, touches on just this point, and there is insight in his comment despite its hostile tone. According to Celsus, the Christians "have revised the gospel in its first written form, three, four, or many times, and have remodeled it so as to be able to refute objections."[23] For this author, Christians produced not multiple gospels but multiple editions of a single original gospel. They did so to preempt the objections to which earlier versions gave rise. As a description of Matthew's procedure vis-à-vis Mark or Luke's vis-à-vis Matthew, Celsus's statement seems to be on target.

However these texts were originally related, all that changes when they are set alongside one another within the fourfold canonical collection. The church's decision to acknowledge four gospels does not simply *recognize* them for what they are; it also *bestows* on each of them its own independent status and validity. If the Gospel of Mark was earlier seen as a preliminary attempt at gospel writing, destined to be absorbed into later and more sophisticated accounts, the collective canonical decision preserves it as a work in its own right. If Luke was once the critic of Matthew, their respective versions of the gospel story now stand side by side. Competing and divergent editions of the same text have become the three "synoptic gospels."

Why "Gospel"?

The term "gospel" occurs sixty times in the Pauline letter collection, although for Paul the gospel is associated with speech rather than writing. The gospel is spoken, preached, proclaimed, evangelized— different terms are used to make the same point.[24] This speech is preceded by written texts in the form of the Scriptures, an essential resource for interpreting the gospel events. It may also be followed by a written text in the form of a Pauline letter that will remind its

23. Quoted in Origen, *Against Celsus* 2.27.
24. The gospel is a message that is spoken (1 Thess. 1:5; 2:2), preached (*kērussein*: Gal. 2:2; 1 Thess. 2:9), proclaimed (*kataggellein*: 1 Cor. 9:14), and evangelized (*euaggelizesthai*: 1 Cor. 9:18; 15:1; 2 Cor. 11:7; Gal. 1:11); thus it is also heard (Gal. 3:2, 5; cf. Eph. 1:13; Col. 1:5) and received (1 Cor. 15:1).

readers of the message once heard and believed. But the gospel itself is not written. It is an interpersonal *event*, a communication in which one speaks and others hear, occurring at a particular time and place. The gospel for Paul is "the gospel of Christ,"[25] for it is Christ who has sent him to preach it, Christ who speaks through it, and Christ who is its content. More specifically, the gospel tells how Christ died for our sins and was raised on the third day, his death underlined by his burial and his resurrection confirmed by his appearing to his followers.[26] A written text that narrates this same train of events is certainly *gospel-like*, but the extension of the term "gospel" into the sphere of writing still needs an explanation.

That explanation may be found in the opening words of the earliest surviving gospel: "The beginning of the Gospel of Jesus Christ."[27] Here, "the Gospel of Jesus Christ" seems to be the original title for the whole of this text—a title later supplanted by the more familiar "Gospel according to Mark."

Mark shares the early view of the gospel as an orally delivered message. At the start of Jesus' ministry, Mark has him returning to Galilee and "proclaiming the gospel of God and saying, 'The time is fulfilled and the kingdom of God has drawn near—repent and believe the gospel!'"[28] The reference to fulfilled time draws attention to an event already encroaching on the present, the dawning of the kingdom of God. If the content of the gospel is the kingdom of God, and if Mark's text is itself gospel, then the two senses of "gospel" must converge: the kingdom of God is what happens in and through Jesus, as narrated by Mark. Of course, Jesus cannot proclaim his own death and resurrection at the start of his ministry, but he can announce a decisive divine intervention whose content is yet to be unveiled.

Elsewhere Mark uses the term "gospel" to refer to the message preached by the apostles after Jesus' departure. He has Jesus speak

25. Rom. 15:19; 1 Cor. 9:12; 2 Cor. 2:12; 9:13; 10:14; Gal. 1:7; Phil. 1:27; 1 Thess. 3:2; cf. 2 Thess. 1:8.
26. 1 Cor. 15:3–9.
27. Mark 1:1.
28. Mark 1:14–15.

of those who leave their families and possessions or lose their lives "for my sake and for the sake of the gospel."[29] Before the end comes, "the gospel must first be preached in all nations."[30] The story of the woman who anointed Jesus' head with precious ointment will be retold "wherever the gospel is preached, in all the world."[31] In the Longer Ending, the risen Lord sends the eleven apostles "into all the world to preach the gospel to the whole creation."[32] At the beginning of Mark's narrative, Jesus preaches the gospel in Galilee; as it draws toward its close, a future is envisaged in which the gospel is preached to all nations, in all the world, and to the whole creation. That is the context in which the evangelist applies the term "gospel" to his own written text, as he announces "the beginning of the Gospel of Jesus Christ."[33] The underlying idea is that his text is the embodiment and continuation of the original apostolic preaching. In writing the gospel, the evangelist ensures that the apostolic testimony is extended to future generations.

Mark was surely not the first to commit to writing sayings and actions attributed to Jesus. In putting this text into something like its present form, he will have had no shortage of earlier written material on which to draw. His own interventions in this earlier material can be clearly identified at many points, and they include the passages where the term "gospel" is highlighted. A traditional saying has Jesus speak of the need for self-sacrifice "for my sake," and Matthew and Luke restore it to its earlier form. It is Mark who has added "and for the sake of the gospel."[34] When Mark entitles his own text "gospel," later evangelists again decline to follow him. Matthew and John refer to their texts not as a gospel but simply as a "book" (*biblos* in Matt. 1:1, perhaps referring only to the genealogy; *biblion* in John 20:30; cf. 21:25). Luke offers his readers a well-structured sequential "account"

29. Mark 8:35; 10:29.
30. Mark 13:10.
31. Mark 14:9.
32. Mark 16:15.
33. Mark 1:1.
34. Mark 8:35; cf. Matt. 16:25; Luke 9:24.

or "narrative" (*diēgēsis*, Luke 1:1; cf. v. 3). Only Mark seems to think that a book of this type should be described as "gospel."

By the mid-second century, Justin Martyr reports that texts that he prefers to describe as "Memoirs of the Apostles" are generally known as "gospels," *euaggelia*.[35] Several of these books were in use in Justin's Roman environment, most prominently Matthew and Luke, and some common term was needed that acknowledged both their similarity and their distinctiveness. No one seems to have thought to describe the gospels as "Lives of Jesus," though there are many points of contact with ancient biographies whose titles follow a "Life of . . ." format.[36] Justin's polysyllabic proposal (*Apomnēmoneumata*, "Memoirs") was never likely to become popular. And so these four "memoirs" or "lives" have been *gospels* ever since.

Why the Evangelists' Names?

Later gospel books like to incorporate their supposed authors' names within their texts. At the end of the main surviving section of the *Gospel of Peter*, we read: "I, Simon Peter, and my brother Andrew took our nets and went to the sea."[37] The *Gospel of Thomas* claims to present its readers with "the secret words which the living Jesus spoke and Didymus Judas Thomas wrote down."[38] A concern with authorship is already perceptible in two of the canonical gospels. In the Longer Ending of John (John 21, a late addition), it is said that the anonymous "disciple whom Jesus loved" is responsible not just for the testimony underlying the gospel but also for writing it.[39] The witness has become an author; tradition will shortly name that author as "John." In the Lukan preface, the evangelist speaks in the first person singular: "It seemed good to me also." This authorial

35. Justin Martyr, *1 Apology* 66.3.
36. That the gospels are typical examples of Greco-Roman biographies has been argued by R. Burridge, *What Are the Gospels?*
37. *Gospel of Peter* 14:60.
38. *Gospel of Thomas*, prologue.
39. John 21:24.

self-introduction seems modest enough when compared to the one found in a contemporary Jewish work that the evangelist may have known: "I, Josephus son of Matthias, a Hebrew by race, a native of Jerusalem and a priest."[40] The evangelist mentions only the name of the dedicatee, Theophilus, and not his own. Yet even this discreet authorial appearance is unprecedented in the older gospel tradition represented by Mark and Matthew. The first individual mentioned by these evangelists is not themselves but "Jesus Christ the Son of God,"[41] "Jesus Christ, son of David, son of Abraham."[42] No authorial persona is allowed to distract attention from him; gospel writing must be anonymous.[43]

This tradition of anonymity is echoed by the gospels' early readers. The text known as the *Didache* (or *The Teaching of the Twelve Apostles*, to give it its full title) may have been compiled only a decade or two after the Gospel of Matthew, with which it has close ties. As he instructs his readers in the name of the twelve apostles, the author echoes Matthew's Sermon on the Mount:

> Do not pray like the hypocrites, but, as the Lord commanded *in his gospel*, pray like this: Our Father in heaven, Hallowed be thy name . . .[44]

> Your prayers and alms and all your acts, perform just as you have them *in the gospel of our Lord*.[45]

The "gospel" here is clearly a written text rather than an oral tradition, and that written text is equally clearly Matthew.[46] Or rather, it is the text we call "Matthew" but which the Didachist knows as "The Gospel of Our Lord," the authoritative text to which "The Teaching of

---

40. *Jewish War* 1.1.
41. Mark 1:1.
42. Matt. 1:1.
43. The original anonymous circulation of the gospels is, however, flatly denied by M. Hengel, *Four Gospels*, 48–56.
44. *Didache* 8.2.
45. *Didache* 15.4.
46. Cf. Matt. 6:1–15.

the Twelve Apostles" must defer. If the Lord commanded something, then it is unimportant to know the name of the scribe who recorded it.

A few decades after the *Didache*, Justin Martyr composed a dialogue between himself and a possibly fictional non-Christian Jew by the name of Trypho. Trypho is presented in a fairly positive light, although his interventions are all too brief in comparison to the verbose Justin character. At one point Trypho indicates a previous interest in Christian faith:

> I regard your rules of conduct *in the so-called "gospel"* as so wonderful and great that I suppose no one is capable of keeping them; for I have read them with care.[47]

Trypho does not specify which rules of conduct he has in mind, but in another context Justin presents a selection of them drawn mainly from the Sermon on the Mount and parallel material elsewhere in Matthew or in Luke.[48] Trypho claims to have engaged with a Christian text, not just an oral tradition, and the text has a title. That title is simply "Gospel." Justin himself can use the same title:

> This saying is written *in the gospel*: "All things are given to me by the Father, and no one knows the Father but the Son, nor the Son but the Father and those to whom the Son reveals him."[49]

The wording differs slightly from the canonical originals, and the saying may have been drawn from either Matthew 11:27 or Luke 10:22 or both. For Justin, however, the saying comes *not* from "Matthew" or "Luke" but from "the gospel." Applied to the Gospel of Matthew in the *Didache*, the term "gospel" may by that point have extended its range to include supplementary gospel material not found in Matthew. To judge from his other citations of Jesus' sayings, Justin's "gospel" is essentially Matthew enhanced by Luke, a "Matthew-plus." (Mark

47. Justin Martyr, *Dialogue with Trypho* 10.2.
48. Justin Martyr, *1 Apology* 15–17.
49. Justin Martyr, *Dialogue with Trypho* 100.1.

and John are barely in evidence, although Justin is probably aware of them, as he is also probably aware of the *Gospel of Peter*.) Yet no individual named authors are in view. At this stage the gospel has its source in the collective apostolic testimony, not in the distinctive perspective of any specific individuals.

So why were individual names attached to these collective apostolic gospel books, with their exclusive focus on the Lord's own words and deeds? What makes the names necessary is the construction of the canonical boundary. A line is drawn around certain texts that definitively separates them from other similar texts. To draw the line at all, the texts it encloses must be identifiable. That is why the first full set of evangelists' names—Matthew, Mark, Luke, and John—appears at precisely the moment when it is first claimed that the church must acknowledge just four gospels. The key figure here is Irenaeus, bishop of Lyons. Around 180 CE, Irenaeus wrote:

> Matthew, among the Hebrews and in their own language, produced a written account of the gospel, while Peter and Paul were in Rome evangelizing and founding the church. After their departure Mark also, the disciple and interpreter of Peter, handed down to us in written form what was preached by Peter. And Luke, the follower of Paul, set down in a book the gospel preached by him. Then John the disciple of the Lord, who reclined upon his breast, published a gospel while living in Ephesus in Asia.[50]

With four named evangelists securely installed, Irenaeus can claim that "it is not possible for the gospels to be either more or fewer in number than they are," and that Christ the divine Word has bestowed on his church a fourfold gospel, a *euaggelion tetramorphon*.[51] Since anonymous gospel books cannot be clearly differentiated, this fourfold gospel requires four named evangelists. Whether Irenaeus's statements preserve any genuine historical information is uncertain. What is more important is to note the profound change that takes place as

---

50. Irenaeus, *Against Heresies* 3.1.1.
51. Irenaeus, *Against Heresies* 3.11.8.

previously anonymous and undifferentiated texts are assigned their own distinct identities.[52]

Why These Four?

There was nothing inevitable about the four-gospel collection. None of the individual evangelists would have anticipated it. If they had done so, they might not have welcomed it: differences between gospels can often be interpreted as active disagreements. But the evangelists were not asked for their opinion on this matter. The fourfold gospel is the collective work of their *readers*, especially the many unknown individuals who made the crucial decisions about which gospel books should be used and read in their own local communities. It was such local decisions that gradually coalesced into an international consensus accepted by the churches of the East and the West.

It might have turned out differently. In view of the preference for Matthew, Mark might have fallen into disuse and disappeared from view. Matthew in turn might have been superseded by Luke; John might have been rejected on the grounds of its supposed incompatibility with earlier gospels. One gospel alone might have been selected, or several earlier gospels might have been combined into a single comprehensive work. The closed canonical collection might have been reopened so as to incorporate a fifth gospel. Indeed, early evidence suggests that just such scenarios actually took place in some local contexts. Any of them might in principle have prevailed—yet they did not. The collective decision went against them.

Mark was not everywhere eclipsed by Matthew; the Longer Ending was added by an editor who wanted to preserve the earlier gospel's independent status. Most readers preferred to see Luke as complementary to Matthew rather than as a competitor. The positive value of the Johannine testimony to Jesus' divinity outweighed concerns about compatibility with other and earlier gospels. Gospel

---

52. For early attestation of evangelists' names in the manuscript tradition, see S. Gathercole, "Titles of the Gospels."

books widely used in some areas failed to establish themselves in others. Circulation of some gospels was deliberately restricted to an elite group conscious of its spiritual superiority to the ordinary Christianity of mainstream churches. One way or another, use or awareness of four gospels must have had a broad-enough basis for Irenaeus's proposal that there *should be* four gospels to seem plausible and reasonable.

Irenaeus himself seems to have had little firsthand knowledge of any gospels other than the four. Texts that circulated widely in, say, Egypt may never have reached him and his fellow Christians in distant Gaul. Arguably, his main concern is not to assert the number four against those who advocate more or fewer gospels, but rather to ensure full recognition for all four texts alike. In Justin, two or three decades earlier, the gospel is essentially Matthew supplemented by Luke, with Mark and John known but barely used. For Irenaeus, Matthew, Mark, Luke, and John possessed equal status. In writing the gospel, they were engaged in a single collective enterprise. And the best evidence of their divine authorization was the fact that these texts were known and recognized throughout the Christian world, in the churches both of the Latin West and the Greek East. The gospel texts that came to be defined as "canonical" were the ones with the deepest roots and widest spread within early Christian usage.

The fourfold canonical gospel might have turned out quite differently, but that does not make it "arbitrary." It took the form it did not because some bishop or council forcibly imposed it on an unwilling or unthinking majority but because of countless small-scale decisions about which texts were to be copied and used and which were to be passed over. Irenaeus's concept of a fourfold gospel offers an interpretation of the general tendency of those small-scale decisions, and his interpretation became normative only because it was and still is accepted as credible and true.

A process of selection took place at every stage in the development of the gospel tradition, and an analogy from an earlier stage may shed light on how the selection process operated. As his gospel draws to a close, the Johannine evangelist tells us that

> Jesus performed many other signs in the presence of his disciples that are not written in this book. But these are written so that you may believe that Jesus is the Christ, the Son of God, and that believing you may have life in his name.[53]

Some signs are selected for inclusion; others are excluded. The first and second of the selected signs are explicitly enumerated: the first sign was the transformation of water into wine, the second the healing of the royal official's son.[54] The enumeration is not maintained, but the selection process continues. The selected signs comprise the healing of the lame man at the pool of Bethesda, the feeding of the five thousand, the walking on water, the bestowal of sight on the man born blind, and the raising of Lazarus. The evangelist (or his source) has selected these seven instances from others that might not have been so effective in pointing the way to eternal life. It would be futile to describe this selection as "arbitrary." The evangelist must have had his reasons for the selection he made, even if these are no longer accessible to us. "These are written so that you may believe" suggests a purposeful selection based on an evaluation of the available material.

Just as the Johannine evangelist selects the seven signs that seem to him most clearly to promote the faith that leads to life, so it is with the collective decision to select four gospels for much the same purpose. The processes by which some gospels were disseminated more rapidly and more widely than others are largely obscure, yet at every stage they must have included evaluations of truth and significance. To commission a new copy of a gospel book for use within one's community is to make a statement about its positive potential for that community's ongoing life. To allow another gospel book to lie unused, or to discard it altogether, is to judge it to

53. John 20:30–31.
54. Cf. John 2:11; 4:54.

be irrelevant, superseded, or misguided. The four-gospel collection represents the sum of local decisions of this kind, extending over more than a century.

In his brief statements about how, when, and where the evangelists came to write their gospels, Irenaeus traces the fourfold gospel back to four individual authors. He is right, of course: without the four author-editors primarily responsible for each of the individual texts, there could be no four-gospel collection. Yet authorial initiative is only part of the story. It is one thing to produce a gospel, but another for it to be recognized as "canonical"—that is, as normative for all present and future Christian communities. Canonical recognition is unlikely to be instantaneous; it requires a process of *discernment* on the part of a gospel's early users. Half a century after Irenaeus, Origen made just this point with great clarity.

Luke's gospel opens with the statement that "many have attempted to compile an account of what has taken place among us." Origen is interested in that word "attempted." Many attempted to write gospels but lacked the divine inspiration the church recognizes in the canonical four. And the church can make this distinction between genuine gospels and attempted ones because its members include "experienced money-changers" practiced in the art of separating the true from the counterfeit:

> Just as, among the people of old, many claimed to prophesy, yet some of them were false prophets while others were true, and the people possessed the gift of discernment of spirits by which the true prophet was distinguished from the false; so now, in the new covenant, many wished to write gospels, but the "experienced money-changers" did not approve them all but selected some of them. The word "attempted" seems to imply an accusation against those who undertook the writing of gospels without the divine gift. For Matthew did not just "attempt" something but wrote by the Holy Spirit, as did Mark and John and also Luke. But as for the ones entitled *Gospel according to the Egyptians* or *Gospel of the Twelve*, their authors indeed "attempted." . . . Indeed, there were "many" who "attempted." For there is a *Gospel according*

to Thomas in circulation, and another *according to Matthias*, and many others. These are the work of those who "attempted." But the church of God selected only the four.[55]

---

55. Origen, *Homilies on Luke* 1. Origen's point is closely related to Calvin's, as summarized by John Webster: "The church's act with respect to the canon is an act of faithful *assent* rather than a self-derived judgment" (*Holy Scripture*, 62 [emphasis original]). That this distinction cannot be demonstrated on neutral terrain does not detract from its significance.

Part 1

---⊕---

Perspectives

At different times and places, the prophet Ezekiel and the seer John experience visions of the throne of God—or is it the throne of Christ? In one case, the throne is also a chariot, identified as such by its wheels and by the fact that it comes to meet the prophet as he meditates in exile by the waters of Babylon. In the other case, the throne stands in heaven. There are no wheels, and the seer must himself be transported into the heavenly world in order to view it. In both cases, the throne is accompanied or surrounded by four living beings, each with four different faces according to the prophet, each with one of the four different faces according to the seer.

For early readers of the canonical gospels, these scriptural images match their own experience of four very different texts that together bear witness to the one Christ. This correspondence between the different faces of heavenly creatures and earthly texts is most clearly visible in the gospels' different starting points. There is a human face, and it corresponds to Matthew's opening genealogy of the Jewish Jesus, descended from David and from Abraham. The lion's face evokes the roar from the desert with which Mark introduces the wild figure of John the Baptist. The face of a calf speaks of sacrifice and the temple, which is where Luke's narrative both begins and ends. The eagle that soars into the heights is the evangelist John, whose gospel opens by bearing witness to the eternal Word who was with God in the beginning and who was God. Like the heavenly creatures, the four evangelists behold the same divine-human reality through different pairs of eyes. These plural yet complementary perspectives are integral to the fourfold gospel, and we may follow the lead of its earlier readers in tracing them back to the divergent gospel openings.

1

The First Gospel:
Jesus the Jew

In most ancient Christian references to the gospels and their origins, the evangelists are listed in the order Matthew–Mark–Luke–John, supposedly the chronological order in which they wrote. In some early Greek and Latin gospel books, the texts themselves are arranged in a different order: Matthew–John–Luke–Mark. Here Mark and John have changed places, with John now promoted to second position in view of his apostolic status and Mark relegated to fourth. Either way, Matthew is presented as the first gospel, the foundation on which the other gospels are built. The question is how and why this gospel attained its foundational status.

In this tradition of placing Matthew first there is one dissenting voice, and it is an important one. Papias, bishop of Hierapolis in Asia Minor, made the first surviving reference to a gospel of Matthew in the early decades of the second century. On the evidence of Eusebius (who quotes him), Papias seems to have referred to Mark

immediately before his reference to Matthew.[1] Papias tells us that
Mark's gospel was based on Peter's preaching, whereas Matthew "set
out the sayings [of Jesus] in the Hebrew language, and each person
translated them as he was able." Eusebius presumably quotes these
two closely related passages in this order because that was their order
within Papias's own text. According to Papias, Mark came first, then
Matthew. Mark wrote "the things said or done by the Lord, though
not in order," whereupon Matthew compiled his own version of the
Lord's sayings. The term "gospel" is not used, but Papias probably
implies that both works presented the sayings of Jesus within a narrative context.

If Papias placed Matthew after Mark, later writers always put
Matthew first. That Mark was actually the first gospel to be written
was the (re)discovery of the nineteenth century. But the reasons for
prioritizing Matthew remain interesting and important, even if they
lack credibility as purely historical claims. In the preface to book 1
of his commentary on Matthew, Origen passes on the tradition he
has received

> about the four gospels which alone are undisputed within the whole
> church under heaven: that the first to be written was the one accord-
> ing to Matthew, formerly a tax collector and later an apostle of Jesus
> Christ, who produced it for believers with a background in Judaism,
> writing in the Hebrew language.[2]

When early Christian writers assume that Matthew wrote his gospel for Jewish Christians, they probably have in mind the opening
genealogy that traces Jesus' ancestry from Abraham onward. According to John Chrysostom, who preached a series of homilies on
Matthew in Antioch in the late fourth century,

> It is said that Matthew, when Jewish believers came and asked him to
> leave in writing what he had said orally, composed his gospel in the

1. Eusebius, *Church History* 3.39.15–16.
2. Origen, *Commentary on Matthew* (preface to book 1) 411.

language of the Hebrews. (And Mark in Egypt at the request of the disciples did likewise.) So Matthew, in what he wrote for the Hebrews, sought to show nothing other than that Christ was descended from Abraham and David. . . . [This] evangelist began with the genealogy; for nothing so pleases a Jew as to learn that the Christ was descended from Abraham and David.[3]

Here too, Matthew is the first of the gospels; Mark in Egypt followed the precedent set by Matthew in Judea. In appealing to the genealogy to establish Matthew's Jewishness, Chrysostom assumes that the distinctive character of an individual gospel is determined by its opening. All four gospels end with passion and Easter narratives, but their starting points are different: the descent from Abraham (Matthew), the ministry of John the Baptist (Mark), Zechariah and Elisabeth (Luke), the eternal Word (John). If we wish to understand what makes Matthew Matthew and not Mark, Luke, or John, we are directed to Matthew's opening; his genealogy establishes the character of his gospel as a whole. Matthew's gospel was placed first because it was believed to have been written for the oldest Christian communities, which were Jewish. And this belief was based largely on an assessment of this gospel's distinctive character, established in the genealogy of Jesus the Jew with which it begins.

Evangelist traditions of this kind were repeated again and again until they were exposed to critical scrutiny from the late eighteenth century onward. From a modern scholarly perspective, these traditions are historically questionable.[4] In reality, the first to write a gospel was Mark rather than Matthew. "Matthew" and "Mark" are just convenient ways of referring to the unknown individuals responsible for compiling these two gospels. "Matthew" used "Mark" as the basis for his own work; he did not write an independent eyewitness account, and he was not an apostle. Like Mark, his primary source, he wrote in Greek, not Hebrew. When Matthew is viewed as the interpreter

---

3. Chrysostom, *Homilies on Matthew* 1.7.
4. But see R. Bauckham, *Jesus and the Eyewitnesses*, 202–39, for a more positive assessment of the Papias traditions.

of Mark, the results are often illuminating, and it is understandable and right that modern scholarly work on the later text should read it in the light of the earlier one.

Within the canonical collection, however, Matthew remains the first gospel. In modern Bibles Matthew still precedes Mark just as surely as Genesis precedes Exodus. In principle an edition of the New Testament might be prepared in which the texts were arranged in chronological order, with 1 Thessalonians at the beginning, James or 2 Peter at the end, and Mark, Matthew, Luke-Acts, and John in between. Yet such an edition would make little sense. The New Testament is an anthology of twenty-seven early Christian writings organized into three distinct collections (Gospels, Pauline Epistles, Catholic Epistles), with important structural roles for Acts in the middle and Revelation at the end. If the collections are dismantled, the New Testament itself disappears; there will no longer be any basis for the boundary that separates the canonical texts from all other Christian texts produced in the period from about 50 to 150 CE. The canonical collections have their own independent reality and integrity, whatever the circumstances that brought them into being. If Mark was written before Matthew, and if Matthew used Mark as his primary source, those interesting and important facts leave Matthew in exactly the same position of priority as before. Matthew is still the first gospel, the foundation of the canonical collection. In spite of their historical shortcomings, those early traditions are making crucial points about this gospel's canonical role.

Matthew's gospel comes first because it presents its readers with a Jewish Jesus who lived and worked within a Jewish context. Jesus does not come from nowhere. According to Matthew, he is the descendant of David in his messianic role, but he is also a descendant of Abraham, a Jew shaped by the whole scriptural story of the people of Israel in their relationship to their God.[5] Matthew has gentile as well as Jewish readers in view. Beginning with a Jewish genealogy, his gospel ends with the command to make disciples of all nations. Yet gentile readers

5. Matt. 1:1.

are brought into the sphere of a Jewish Jesus, a Jesus who opens up to the whole world the riches of Jewish scriptural tradition—the law and the prophets. Matthew's Jesus is the world's savior not *in spite of* being a Jew but *as* a Jew. Matthew comes first in the canonical collection because—in the view of his early readers, who put him there—his emphasis on Jesus' Jewishness is the key to understanding who Jesus is. Then as now, there were Christians who preferred a purely heavenly Jesus untainted by any merely human origins, especially Jewish ones. In placing Matthew first, the architects of the canon declare this un-Jewish and purely heavenly Jesus to be a fantasy.

So Matthew's Jesus is first and foremost a Jew. But what does it mean to be a Jew? How is this contested term to be understood, and how does it apply to Jesus? These are the questions that the evangelist addresses in his opening genealogy.

The Messiah's Double Origin

The Gospel of Matthew opens with the two words *biblos geneseōs*. In themselves these words might be translated "book of Genesis." Indeed, this phrase is taken straight from the book of Genesis in its Greek form, where it introduces the genealogy that runs from Adam through Seth down to Noah and his sons.[6] This scriptural language suggests to the evangelist a title for his opening section: "The book of the genesis of Jesus Christ, son of David, son of Abraham."[7] The Greek term *genesis* speaks of the process that brings something into being—the origin, source, or beginning that produces it and enables it to be what it is. Depending on the context, it might be translated either "genealogy" or "birth." Both these senses are present in Matthew's first chapter. In "the book of the genesis of Jesus Christ," *genesis* clearly means "genealogy." Jesus is the son of David and of Abraham, and a full, carefully crafted genealogy follows directly from this opening statement.

6. Gen. 5:1–32.
7. Matt. 1:1.

At the close of that genealogy, we read of another, related genesis: "The genesis of Jesus Christ was like this," or, "The birth of Jesus Christ took place in this way."[8] This statement introduces Matthew's account of the events that follow Jesus' miraculous conception and his birth in Bethlehem. So Matthew's Jesus has a double genesis or origin: he is the product of a long line of ancestors, and he is also the child of Mary, miraculously conceived through the Holy Spirit. The genesis of Jesus Christ is his genealogy, from Abraham through David to Joseph, and it is also his birth from Mary.

There is a problem here. The genealogy and the birth seem to contradict each other; more precisely, the miraculous birth seems to cancel out the genealogy. At its close, the genealogy states that "Eleazar was the father of Matthan, Matthan the father of Jacob, Jacob the father of Joseph, the husband of Mary, from whom was born Jesus called the Christ."[9] That "from whom" refers to Mary alone. Joseph is not a father but a husband; the long list of fathers comes to a halt with Joseph's own father, Jacob. We expect to read that, as Jacob fathered Joseph, so Joseph fathered Jesus called the Christ. That would fit the context perfectly, yet the evangelist suddenly abandons his list of fathers to focus on the mother of a fatherless child. Joseph is named only to be instantly marginalized. He is a husband but not a father; the child borne by his wife is not his. Unsurprisingly, he reacts negatively:

> While his mother Mary was engaged to Joseph, before they came together, she was found to be pregnant by the Holy Spirit. Joseph her husband, being a just man and not wanting to disgrace her, decided to end the engagement quietly. As he reflected on this, an angel of the Lord appeared to him in a dream and said, "Joseph son of David, do not fear to take Mary as your wife, for what she has conceived is from the Holy Spirit."[10]

8. Matt. 1:18.
9. Matt. 1:15–16.
10. Matt. 1:18–20.

So Joseph goes ahead with his marriage and accepts his marginal status as the husband of a woman whose child was conceived without him. The evangelist does not explain how Jesus can be the son of David as Joseph is the son of David. He might have said that Joseph adopted Jesus as his own son, but he does not do so. Indeed, unlike Luke and John,[11] Matthew never speaks of Joseph as Jesus' father. When the magi arrive in Bethlehem with their gifts, they see "the child with Mary his mother."[12] Joseph is entirely out of the picture. His role is to be a protective one. Acting in obedience to an angel's instruction, he takes "the child and his mother" to Egypt to escape Herod's murderous rage and brings them back to the land of Israel after Herod's death.[13] Joseph seems more like a guardian than a father; the child is never described as *his* child. Yet Joseph's relationship to the child must still be important for the evangelist, if the genealogy is truly the genealogy of the Messiah. The figures it lists must somehow be Jesus' ancestors, not just Joseph's, and they must be Jesus' ancestors *through* Joseph.

Matthew's Jesus has a double origin or genesis. He is a Jew, a descendant of Abraham, the product of a long succession of generations. That is the heritage he receives from Joseph. Yet his mother Mary conceives him through the Holy Spirit and without Joseph, so that Jesus is not just a son of Abraham or a son of David but also "Immanuel, God-with-us."[14] The miraculous conception breaks the genealogical chain, but the evangelist still devotes twice as much space to the genealogy as to the conception and its aftermath.

Is the evangelist simply confused? Is he trying to combine two independent and incompatible traditions about where Jesus comes from, one taking a standard genealogical route, the other claiming a miracle? That would be a possible conclusion but not a necessary one. We must look more closely at the genealogy itself for clues as to how it might still be valid, even when the final link in the genealogical chain is apparently broken.

11. Luke 2:41–48; John 1:45; 6:42.
12. Matt. 2:11.
13. Matt. 2:13–14, 20–21.
14. Cf. Matt. 1:23.

Genealogy as Narrative

On closer inspection, the genealogy is not just about family or descent or heredity; rather, it is a highly condensed summary of the scriptural history of Israel. Jesus is miraculously conceived, but he is also the product and goal of Israel's history as recounted in the scriptural narratives. Just as he is shaped in Mary's womb, so he is also shaped by a story. The story begins with the book of Genesis:

> Abraham fathered Isaac, Isaac fathered Jacob, Jacob fathered Judah and his brothers, Judah fathered Perez and Zerah by Tamar . . .[15]

These statements refer not just to genealogical facts but to entire sections of the Genesis narrative. The Greek verb *egennēsen* refers to an event of fatherhood: Abraham *fathered* Isaac. That event occurred when

> the LORD visited Sarah as he had said, and the LORD did to Sarah as he had promised. And Sarah conceived and bore Abraham a son in his old age at the time of which God had spoken to him. Abraham called the name of his son who was born to him Isaac.[16]

In its context in Genesis, Isaac's birth is not an isolated event. The whole Abraham narrative has led up to it. Abraham is introduced as the bearer of divine promises. God will make of him a great nation, as innumerable as the stars in the sky or the grains of sand on the seashore; in him all the families of the earth will be blessed.[17] Yet these long-term promises cannot be fulfilled unless Abraham produces a son, and he and Sarah are an elderly, childless couple. The tension between the promise and its apparently impossible fulfillment runs throughout the Abraham narrative. When Abraham and his nephew Lot part company, the narrator rules out the possibility that Lot might be adopted as Abraham's son, heir to the promise of the great nation.

15. Matt. 1:2–3.
16. Gen. 21:1–3.
17. Gen. 12:2–3; 15:5; 22:17.

Lot does eventually become the father of not one nation but two, Moab and Ammon, but the horrifying context of violence and incest shows that he has no part in the promise to Abraham.[18] Unlike Lot, Ishmael is genuinely Abraham's son, but his birth to the slave-girl Hagar enrages Sarah, who eventually has them driven out into the arid and inhospitable wilderness. Ishmael will eventually become a father of twelve, but he is not the chosen heir.[19] Even after the birth of Isaac, the divine promise is once again thrown into question as Abraham prepares to obey the command to offer him up as a sacrifice.[20] In the simple statement that Abraham fathered Isaac, Matthew summarizes the Genesis Abraham narrative in its entirety. Unless and until Abraham becomes the father of Isaac and Isaac is preserved to become a father in his turn, the divine promise is in jeopardy. Without Abraham, Isaac, and Jacob there would be no people of Israel and no Israelite named Jesus the Christ.

Isaac fathered Jacob, and Jacob fathered Judah and his brothers. Matthew's brief statements again cover great expanses of the Genesis narrative. They also offer an interpretation of that narrative, one that focuses on Judah rather than Joseph among the sons of Jacob. In the final chapters of Genesis, the central figure is Joseph. His father's favorite, hated by his brothers, Joseph dreams of his own dominance over his family, and the Genesis narrator tells how his dreams were fulfilled—in Egypt, the place of refuge that later became the place of oppression. Joseph is a spectacular figure who puts the rest of his family in the shade. Yet Matthew's genealogy does not state that Jacob fathered Joseph and his brothers; it is Judah who is mentioned by name. Joseph son of Jacob is absent from Matthew's succinct summary of the scriptural narrative, perhaps to create space for a later Joseph son of Jacob, husband of Mary.

At this point in the genealogy, individuals are referred to by name who are not part of the strict genealogical succession from father to

18. Gen. 19:30–38.
19. Gen. 21:8–21; 25:12–18.
20. Gen. 22.

son. There is a brother, and there is also a mother: "Judah fathered
Perez and Zerah by Tamar, Perez fathered Hezrom . . ."[21] The naming
of a mother and a brother is unexpected. Sarah and Rebecca, Ishmael
and Esau have not been mentioned, yet the evangelist here chooses to
name a much less well-known mother and brother alongside the father
and son. The extra names refer us to the story in Genesis 38 of the
patriarch Judah's seduction by his doubly widowed daughter-in-law
Tamar, whose legitimate claim on him Judah finally acknowledges.
Why would Matthew draw attention to this embarrassing story, which
is as alien to the social conventions of his own time as it is to ours?
Tamar's unexpected appearance may foreshadow Mary's, but there is
more to it than that. In naming Tamar alongside the patriarch Judah,
the genealogy makes explicit its relationship to the scriptural narrative. If the evangelist had written only "Judah fathered Perez," that
would be just another link in the long genealogical chain. By adding
that "Judah fathered Perez and Zerah by Tamar," the evangelist draws
us into the world of the Genesis story.

The birth of these twins to Judah and Tamar is also the point
at which the evangelist exits the Genesis story. The obscure names
that follow—Hezron and Ram, Amminadab and Nahshon, and so
on—are drawn from the Judahite genealogy in 1 Chronicles 2, which
is concerned mainly to trace the ancestry of King David. But here
too the evangelist adds in female characters to ensure that his genealogy remains connected to the scriptural narrative as a whole.
We learn that "Salmon fathered Boaz *by Rahab* and Boaz fathered
Obed *by Ruth*."[22] Rahab was the prostitute who gave shelter to the
Israelite spies in Jericho and whose reward was to be spared along
with her family when the city was destroyed.[23] She is commended
for her faith in the Letter to the Hebrews[24] and for her works in the
Letter of James.[25] The book of Joshua tells us that Rahab "dwelt in

21. Matt. 1:3.
22. Matt. 1:5.
23. Josh. 2:1–21; 6:22–25.
24. Heb. 11:31.
25. James 2:25.

Israel to this day, because she hid the messengers whom Joshua sent to spy out Jericho."[26] So Rahab was integrated into the people of Israel. Did she abandon her former disreputable profession and marry an Israelite? Matthew thinks she did. If "Salmon fathered Boaz by Rahab," then Rahab has presumably married into the line of Judah's descendants and David's ancestors. Perhaps Matthew imagined that her husband, Salmon, was one of the two unnamed spies to whom she had given sanctuary. They are described in the book of Joshua as "young men," and they are given the task of rescuing Rahab and her family from the doomed city,[27] so romance and marriage might well have seemed plausible to the evangelist. In any case, Rahab too becomes a mother in Israel.

Rahab was the mother of Boaz, "Boaz fathered Obed by Ruth," and, three generations later, "David fathered Solomon by the wife of Uriah."[28] The evangelist completes his unique quartet of female characters, ancestors or foremothers of the Messiah: not Sarah, Rebecca, Leah, and Rachel, but Tamar, Rahab, Ruth, and Bathsheba. Each of these women brings to the genealogy her own story, which is also the story of the men in her life: Judah and his sons, Salmon the spy, Boaz the wealthy and honorable farmer, Uriah the tragic victim of royal jealousy, and King David with his disastrous family life.

Why does the evangelist evoke these not-always-edifying stories? What light do they shed on the intention underlying the genealogy as a whole, with its strangely indirect link to Jesus himself? We must look still more closely at the evangelist's scriptural sources.

The Sacred Story and Its Shadow

In constructing his genealogy, Matthew has drawn freely not only from his knowledge of scriptural narrative but also from the genealogies at the beginning of 1 Chronicles (see table 1.1). Comparison of

26. Josh. 6:25.
27. Josh. 6:23.
28. Matt. 1:5–6.

Table 1.1

1 Chronicles 2:3–15	Matthew 1:3–7
Sons of Judah: Er and Onan and Shelah, these three were born to him by Bathshua the Canaanite. And Er, Judah's firstborn, was wicked in the LORD's eyes, and he slew him.	Judah
And *Tamar* his daughter-in-law [Greek: "bride"] bore to him Perez and Zerah. The sons of Judah were five in all.	fathered Perez and Zerah *by Tamar*,
Sons of Perez: Hezron and Hamul. And the sons of Zerah: Zimri and Ethan and Heman and Calcol and Dara: five of them in all. . . .	and Perez fathered Hezrom,
And the sons of Hezron that were born to him: Jerahmeel, Ram, Chelubai, and Aram.*	and Hezrom fathered
Aram fathered Amminadab,	Aram, and Aram fathered Amminadab,
and Amminadab fathered Nahshon, prince of the sons of Judah,	and Amminadab fathered Nahshon,
and Nahshon fathered Salma,	and Nahshon fathered Salmon,
and Salma fathered Boaz,	and Salmon fathered Boaz *by Rahab*,
and Boaz fathered Obed,	and Boaz fathered Obed *by Ruth*,
and Obed fathered Jesse,	and Obed fathered Jesse,
and Jesse fathered Eliab his firstborn, Abinadab the second, Shimea the third, Nethanel the fourth, Raddai the fifth, Ozem the sixth, David the seventh.†	and Jesse fathered David the king,

1 Chronicles 3:1–10	
These are the sons of David who were born to him in Hebron. . . . And these were born to him in Jerusalem: Shimea, Shobab, Nathan, and	and David
Solomon, four by Bathshua [Bathsheba] the daughter of Ammiel. . . .	fathered Solomon *by Uriah's wife*,
And the son of Solomon was Rehoboam, Abijah his son . . .	and Solomon fathered Rehoboam, and Rehoboam fathered Abijah . . .

* Aram's name occurs in the Septuagint but not in the Hebrew.
† This section of the Judahite genealogy also occurs in Ruth 4:18–22. While the evangelist may have been aware of this, the Chronicles genealogies are likely to have been his main source. Matthew's reference to Tamar is suggested by 1 Chron. 2:4, and his list of descendants of David is drawn from 1 Chron. 3:10–16.

Matthew 1:3–7 with 1 Chronicles 2:3–15 and 3:1–10 sheds light on what the evangelist is trying to achieve as he opens his gospel with a genealogy. Most obviously, he constructs out of his diverse source material a single, orderly, and purely vertical line of descent.

All genealogies are "vertical" in the sense that they trace the progression of successive generations; as each father produces a son, one generation gives way to the next. Yet parents usually produce more than one child, and genealogies can therefore be extended horizontally to include any number of sons and daughters from whom further vertical lines of descent may spring. The Chronicles genealogies on which Matthew draws contain frequent lists of brothers, with occasional sisters added in too. The five sons of Judah and of his son Zerah are listed by name; so too are David's brothers and sisters, his four sons by Bathsheba, the six sons by six mothers born to him in Hebron, and the nine further sons and a daughter born in Jerusalem. These genealogies also contain purely vertical sections, however, and Matthew takes over one such section almost word for word.

Chronicles lists the six generations from Aram (great-grandson of Judah) to Jesse (father of David) in pure father-to-son sequence, without reference to additional brothers and sisters.[29] Matthew not only incorporates this passage into his own genealogy; he also uses its key term to organize his genealogy as a whole. In the Chronicles passage the relationship of father to son is conveyed by the single Greek word *egennēsen* ("fathered"). In 1 Chronicles 2 there are seven successive occurrences of this *egennēsen* formula. In Matthew 1 there are thirty-nine of them. The result is a strong sense of cohesion and an equally strong sense of direction. The Chronicles genealogies seem to be going nowhere in particular. They are collections of miscellaneous information with no clear chronological framework, and in most cases they come to an end without reaching any obvious goal. If there is a single concern, it is to remember and record the sacred past of the twelve tribes of Israel. Matthew's genealogy is different.

29. 1 Chron. 2:10–12.

There is no interest in the twelve tribes; instead, the sacred scriptural past is reshaped so that it points toward a single goal, the birth of the Messiah. Everything superfluous has been cut out.

It is all the more striking, then, that Matthew retains two of the women mentioned in the Chronicler's Judahite genealogies and adds two more: Judah fathered Perez and Zerah *by Tamar*, Salmon fathered Boaz *by Rahab*, Boaz fathered Obed *by Ruth*, David fathered Solomon *by Uriah's wife*. Tamar is mentioned in Matthew's source, but Matthew is responsible for adding Rahab and Ruth and identifying Bathsheba as "Uriah's wife." In each case these references call to mind a scriptural narrative, and the evangelist must have his reasons for highlighting these stories and not others. As we have seen, Matthew's genealogy is a summary of the history of Israel as recorded in Scripture. The question is whether we can see the four women's stories as some kind of key to that greater story.

The reference to "Uriah's wife" is striking. In the scriptural narrative, Bathsheba is referred to as "Uriah's wife" only so long as the focus is on David's guilt. After Uriah dies fighting the Ammonites and David has hastily married Bathsheba, David's crimes are exposed by the prophet Nathan:

> You have struck Uriah the Hittite with the sword and his wife you have taken as your own wife, killing him with the sword of the Ammonites. So now the sword shall not leave your house, because you have despised me by taking *the wife of Uriah the Hittite* to be your own wife.[30]

Shortly afterward, "the LORD struck the child that *Uriah's wife* bore to David, and it became sick," dying soon after in spite of David's prayer and fasting.[31] That is the last time that Bathsheba is referred to as "Uriah's wife." After that she recovers her own name as her new marriage is recognized:

30. 2 Sam. 12:9–10.
31. 2 Sam. 12:15–23.

David comforted *Bathsheba his wife*, and he came to her and lay
with her, and she conceived and bore a son, and he called his name
Solomon. And the LORD loved him.[32]

At the time of Solomon's birth, it seems that David and Bathsheba
are lawfully married; David's guilt has been forgiven, and there is no
further mention of Uriah. But Matthew sees things differently. David
is a key figure in his genealogy, for the Messiah himself is to be a son
of David. And yet, "David fathered Solomon *by the wife of Uriah*."[33]
Uriah is not so easily forgotten. For the evangelist, Solomon's birth
takes place under the dark shadow of adultery and murder.

Looking back, we see the same shadow hanging over the three earlier women the evangelist names as he retraces King David's descent
from the patriarch Judah. Tamar deceives and seduces her father-in-
law by acting the part of a prostitute in a desperate attempt to get
justice from him. Rahab does not act a part; she is a prostitute by
profession. Ruth might seem to be a less controversial figure, yet she
attempts to seduce Boaz to compel him to marry her. Neither the
evangelist nor the scriptural stories themselves impute any blame to
these women; they are all presented positively and sympathetically.
Yet their presence in a genealogy is an embarrassment. The entire
tribe of Judah, after whom the Jewish people is named, traces its
origin to the shameful liaison between the patriarch Judah and the
disguised Tamar. King David has among his immediate ancestors two
other foreign women whose sexual conduct is, at the very least, out
of step with conventional morality. The ghost of Uriah the Hittite
continues to haunt David's descendants. Matthew's genealogy seems
intended to disturb his readers. It does not present the scriptural history of Israel as an inspirational story of faith and salvation. Rather,
it directs attention to the shadow side of that history.

The shadow lengthens and deepens in the central section of the
genealogy, which traces the succession of kings that arose out of

32. 2 Sam. 12:24.
33. Matt. 1:6.

David's relationship with Uriah's wife and that ended with the national catastrophe of exile in Babylon. For the evangelist, the exile is a crucially significant event; the full phrase "deportation to Babylon" occurs no less than four times in his otherwise economical genealogy, twice within its main body and twice in its concluding enumeration of three sets of fourteen generations.[34] Up to this point the listing of the generations before and after David has proceeded smoothly, without any break or change of format (see table 1.2). At the exile, the list comes to an abrupt halt. After the exile, a new start is needed:

> Hezekiah fathered Manasseh, Manasseh fathered Amon, Amon fathered Josiah, Josiah fathered Jechoniah and his brothers at the time of the deportation to Babylon. After the deportation to Babylon, Jechoniah fathered Salathiel . . .[35]

According to the evangelist, each section of the genealogy contains fourteen generations, from Abraham to David, from David to the exile, and from the exile to Jesus.[36] A key role is assigned to an otherwise obscure figure, Jechoniah, also known as Jehoiakin, the eighteen-year-old son of Jehoiakim who ruled for just three months before surrendering himself and the royal family to the Babylonian invaders.[37] Exiled to Babylon, Jehoiakin/Jechoniah endured thirty-seven years of imprisonment before being released.[38] He is therefore remembered as "Jechoniah the captive."[39] For Matthew's enumeration to work, Jechoniah must be counted twice: as the last member of the central section of the list and as the first member of its final section. (Otherwise there will be thirteen rather than fourteen generations in the final part of the genealogy.)[40] Jechoniah is assigned a dual role within Israel's national

34. Matt. 1:11–12, 17.
35. Matt. 1:10–12.
36. Matt. 1:17.
37. 2 Kings 24:8–17.
38. 2 Kings 25:27–30.
39. 1 Chron. 3:17.
40. In which case Matthew may have committed "a mathematical blunder" (W. D. Davies and D. C. Allison, *Matthew*, 1:186).

Table 1.2

(1) Fourteen generations from Abraham to David (Matt. 1:17; 1 Chron. 1:28–2:15)	(2) Fourteen generations from David to the exile (Matt. 1:17; 1 Chron. 3:10–16)	(3) Fourteen generations from the exile to the Christ (Matt. 1:17; cf. 1 Chron. 3:17–19; Hag. 1:1, 12)
1. **Abraham**	1. **Solomon**	1. **Jechoniah**
2. Isaac	2. Rehoboam	2. Salathiel
3. Jacob	3. Abijah	3. Zerubbabel
4. Judah/Tamar	4. Asa	4. Abiud
5. Perez	5. Jehoshaphat	5. Eliakim
6. Hezron	6. Joram	6. Azor
7. Ram	[Ahaziah]	7. Zadok
8. Amminadab	[Joash]	8. Achim
9. Nahshon	[Amaziah]	9. Eliud
10. Salmon/Rahab	7. Uzziah	10. Eleazar
11. Boaz/Ruth	8. Jotham	11. Matthan
12. Obed	9. Ahaz	12. Jacob
13. Jesse	10. Hezekiah	13. Joseph [Mary]
14. **David**/Bathsheba	11. Manasseh	14. **Jesus called Christ**
	12. Amon	
	13. Josiah	
	[Jehoiakim]	
	14. **Jechoniah**	

The first two columns are continuous, whereas the third represents a new start after the exile—hence the repetition of Jechoniah's name.

story as the evangelist understands it. At the time of the exile, he is the last authentic king of Judah. After the exile, he is the first in a new, nonroyal line consisting largely of unknown figures whose names and stories are nowhere to be found in Scripture. Israel's sacred story seems to have come to an end. It lies in an ever-receding past, recorded in Scripture but a living reality only in recollection. The story that began with Abraham's election ends with Jehoiakin's humiliation.

Why did the story turn out like this? In listing the kings of Judah, David's descendants, Matthew will have been in no doubt about the answer. The scriptural narrative passes its verdict on these individuals with monotonous regularity. Of the fourteen named here, eight are said to have "done evil in the sight of the LORD."[41] Manasseh,

41. Solomon (1 Kings 11:6), Rehoboam (1 Kings 14:22), Abijam (1 Kings 15:3), Joram (2 Kings 8:18), Ahaz (2 Kings 16:2), Manasseh (2 Kings 21:2, 9–15), Amon

renegade son of Hezekiah, comes in for particularly sharp criticism. During his fifty-five-year reign, Manasseh led his people astray from the one true God. The divine verdict on king and people is damning and unqualified:

> And I will cast off the remnant of my heritage, and give them into the hand of their enemies, and they will become a prey and a spoil to all their enemies, because they have done what is evil in my sight and have provoked me to anger, since the day their fathers came out of Egypt, even to this day.[42]

In the fate of Jehoiakin some eighty years later, these threats come to fruition. The king and his subjects go into exile; the land promised to Abraham and his descendants is forfeited. In giving such prominence to the exile, Matthew's genealogy suggests that the sacred history recorded in Israel's scriptures does not have the power to regenerate itself. Rather, it awaits some decisive event in which God will act to save his people. The postexilic generations stand at the intersection of catastrophe and hope.

The Genealogy of Jesus the Messiah

At this point we begin to glimpse an answer to the main question raised by the genealogy—the question of why it is there at all, given that it remains suspended at the figure of Joseph, who was *not* the father of Jesus. The question has negative and positive aspects. On the negative side, why is Joseph not Jesus' father? On the positive side, how is Joseph's genealogy also Jesus' genealogy, as the evangelist insists that it is?

Though addressed by an angel as "son of David,"[43] Joseph is not and cannot be Jesus' father. Why? Following the genealogy, we read

---

(2 Kings 21:20), Jehoiakin (2 Kings 24:9). Positive verdicts, sometimes qualified, are recorded for Asa (1 Kings 15:11), Jehoshaphat (1 Kings 22:43), Uzziah (2 Kings 15:3), Hezekiah (2 Kings 18:3), and Josiah (2 Kings 22:2).

42. 2 Kings 21:14–15 (RSV).

43. Matt. 1:20.

that Joseph became reconciled to his exclusion from paternity when the realities of his situation were laid bare in a dream.[44] In obeying the angel's command that the child should be named Jesus, Joseph shows that he has accepted and understood his own marginalization. The child is to be named Jesus because "he will save his people from their sins."[45] "His people" are the people of Israel, descended from Abraham, Isaac, and Jacob, just as Joseph is. This people is a sinful people, and its sin is pervasive, spreading down through the generations. The case of David and Uriah's wife is symptomatic; it is not an unfortunate exception to an otherwise outstanding record of piety and integrity. On a broader canvas, the exile is equally symptomatic. Indeed, David's sin and the later fate of the nation are combined in the greatest of the penitential psalms: Psalm 51, the *Miserere*. This psalm is ascribed to David, on the occasion "when Nathan the prophet came to him, after he had gone in to Bathsheba."[46] Yet the psalm closes with a prayer reflecting a much later exilic setting: "Do good to Zion in thy good pleasure; rebuild the walls of Jerusalem."[47] The penitent David becomes a model for later generations who live in the aftermath of the nation's destruction.

In view of this history, Joseph cannot be the father of a Messiah who "will save his people from their sins." This history cannot deliver itself from the burden of its past. The coming of the Messiah must be the act of God. As the prophet and the angel announce, his name will be "Immanuel, God-with-us."[48]

And yet the evangelist opens his gospel with a genealogy of Jesus, not just of Joseph. Jesus does not derive any part of his genetic makeup from Joseph, but Joseph does embody the particular history that the newborn child will enter and be shaped by. Just as the adult Jesus will later submit himself to John's baptism of repentance, so the messianic child is subject to a history that can only be understood

44. Matt. 1:19–23.
45. Matt. 1:21.
46. Ps. 51, title (RSV); cf. 2 Sam. 12:13.
47. Ps. 51:18 (RSV).
48. Matt. 1:23.

as a call to repentance. He does not evade or transcend this history as though it were alien to him, for the history that shaped the earlier postexilic generations is *his* history too. He could not save his people from their sins if the historic people of Israel were not "his people" and if he did not himself enter the sphere pervaded by "their sins." He saves his people from within their situation, not as a *deus ex machina* from without. In order to transform a context of alienation from God, in which the divine grace is no more than a recollection and hope, he must himself be formed by that context.

It is not surprising that the evangelist's early readers assumed that the apostle Matthew was writing for his fellow Jews, in their own land and in their own language. These readers noted that genealogy is a distinctively Jewish concern and that this genealogy starts from Abraham, father of the Jewish people, rather than anticipating Luke by going back to Adam, father of the whole human race. They noted that the name "Jesus" refers to the salvation of "his people." They knew, of course, that at the end of this gospel the risen Lord sends out the Eleven to "make disciples of all nations . . . teaching them to observe all that I have commanded you."[49] They did not suppose that a gospel originally addressed to Jewish believers was irrelevant to non-Jews. Yet no attentive reader of Matthew could suppose that the Jewish scriptural heritage can simply be consigned to the past and forgotten. A Jesus lacking a Jewish formation would require a quite different kind of gospel.

Matthew's gospel bears witness to a Jewish Jesus whose person and work are shaped by his people's history as interpreted in the scriptural record. This gospel was placed first in the canonical collection because its early readers were convinced by its fundamental claim: salvation has come to the world in the person of a Jew.

---

49. Matt. 28:19–20.

2

The Second Gospel:
Preparing the Way

For many of its early readers, the text we know as "the Gospel according to Matthew" was simply "the Gospel." When the author of the *Didache* instructs his readers to pray "as the Lord commanded in his Gospel," it is Matthew's version of the Lord's Prayer that he has in mind: "Our Father in heaven . . ."[1] Yet there was also an earlier, shorter version of the Gospel in existence, the one that was generally attributed to Mark. In some early Christian communities, Matthew may have replaced Mark. In others, Mark must have continued in use alongside Matthew. As still more gospel literature began to circulate, it became increasingly clear that the Lord's Gospel consisted of more than one text. The selection process that resulted in the four-gospel collection may have had its roots in the early coexistence of Matthew and Mark.

Mark, then, played a key role in establishing a plural gospel; or rather, Mark's loyal readers did so, simply by continuing to use the

1. *Didache* 8.2; cf. Matt. 6:9.

older text in spite of the general preference for Matthew's newer and more comprehensive one. But the decision to acknowledge more than one version of the same story needed to be justified, especially when the number of widely accepted versions grew to four. Faced with this issue, it occurred to someone—Irenaeus or an unknown predecessor—to turn to the book of the prophet Ezekiel.

The Four Faces of the Gospel

A priest among the exiles in Babylon, Ezekiel receives his prophetic calling by way of a surreal and spectacular vision that he describes in intricate detail. By the end of his first chapter, it is clear that what he sees is a chariot attended by strange angelic beings, and that this chariot serves as a mobile throne for the Lord. Yet it takes some time for the full picture to emerge. Unlike the prophet Isaiah, who sees the Lord "high and lifted up" right at the start of his vision,[2] Ezekiel becomes fixated on the chariot and its attendants and raises his eyes to view the heavenly throne and its occupant only as his description draws to a close. At the start of the vision "the likeness of four living creatures" emerges from a fiery cloud. Although essentially human in form, each of the four creatures possesses four wings, four faces, and four sides, each side equipped with its own pair of hands. Their human faces are turned toward the prophet, but he also notes the faces of a lion and a calf to right and left and an eagle's face behind. The four living creatures and the wheels they accompany are in constant motion, up and down, to and fro. The wheels are colossal, and their rims are full of eyes.[3]

What in this vision might have interested an early Christian reader? High above the wheels and the creatures, a voice issues forth from the One seated on the throne, who is human in appearance. In the cryptic language of the prophet himself, there sat "upon the likeness of a throne a likeness as of the form of a man."[4] God himself cannot be seen; as

2. Isa. 6:1.
3. Ezek. 1:5–18.
4. Ezek. 1:26.

Moses was told, "No one shall see me and live."[5] For the early Christian reader, a visible manifestation of God could only be a prefiguring of Christ, the one in whom the hidden God is presented to human view.[6] Given that interpretation of Ezekiel's vision, the question of why so much attention is given to the four creatures with their four faces, rather than to the enthroned Christ, might then arise. Presumably it was *necessary* for the prophet to fix his attention on the lesser beings before lifting up his eyes to the One enthroned above. If so, then this suggests an analogy. Just as the prophet beholds the exalted Christ only by focusing first on the four living creatures, so we behold him only by attending to the four gospels. And just as Christ presented himself to the prophet by way of the four-wheeled chariot and its four attendants, so he presents himself to us by way of a fourfold gospel and four evangelists.

The crucial point is still to come. The four living creatures are identical, whereas the four gospels differ. (Without that difference we would have not four gospels but four copies of a single gospel.) Among Ezekiel's various groups of four, there is one that reflects this difference. Four wheels are accompanied by four living creatures, each with four wings, four sides, and four faces—and the faces *differ*. And so the differences between Matthew, Mark, Luke, and John were seen to be mirrored in the differences between the living creatures' four faces: one human, the others those of a lion, a calf, and an eagle. Indeed, the two sequences could be aligned; thus, Matthew is paired with the human face or human figure, Mark with that of a lion, Luke with that of a calf, and John with that of an eagle. (Those, at least, are the pairings proposed in the best-known version of this scheme, which goes back to Jerome in the late fourth century.)[7] The difference between the four names is matched by the difference between the four faces, and both differences represent the differences between the texts themselves. Perhaps it is surprising that

5. Exod. 33:20.
6. This interpretation of Ezekiel's vision is already present in Irenaeus, *Against Heresies* 4.20.10.
7. Jerome outlines this scheme on a number of occasions—for example, in the preface to his *Commentary on Matthew*. In an earlier version of the scheme, the lion represents John, and the eagle Mark; see Irenaeus, *Against Heresies* 3.11.8.

the church should use four different versions of the same story. Ezekiel was no doubt equally surprised to see four different faces on a single heavenly being. For both the prophet and the church, the fourfold form is as it is because God willed it to be so: that is the claim. God willed a variegated creation in which humans, lions, calves, and eagles all have their place. That is also true of the new creation realized through Christ. It seems that the biblical God likes diversity.

Literal-minded scholars have often regarded this traditional defense of the four-gospel collection as arbitrary and artificial. Actually it is remarkably *un*arbitrary, given that the idea of a fourfold gospel is unlikely ever to have entered the head of the prophet Ezekiel. According to Jerome and others, the human face is assigned to Matthew because this gospel opens with Jesus' human genealogy. The eagle's face is assigned to John because, in contrast to Matthew, this gospel soars into the heights of the divine sphere in which the Word was with God in the beginning. And so the two "apostolic" gospels bear witness respectively to one who is human (but also divine) and to one who is divine (but also human). That leaves the two "postapostolic" gospels attributed to Mark and Luke. Luke begins and ends in the Jerusalem temple; the sacrificial calf is therefore appropriate to him. Mark begins in the desert, where animal life is mostly wild rather than domesticated. The desert is the setting for the ministry of John the Baptist, the wildest and least domesticated of all biblical characters. His is the voice—which Jerome compares to a lion's roar—that cries out in the wilderness. In the wilderness Jesus is tempted, and there he is "with the wild animals," including, no doubt, lions.[8] As a symbol of Mark's wild opening, the lion is a perfect fit.

The Voice in the Desert

In Mark, Jesus' messianic vocation is traced back to the ministry of John the Baptist. John was also given an important role in Matthew,

8. Mark 1:13.

although there the account of his ministry is preceded by an elaborate genealogy and infancy narrative. In Matthew's densely populated opening chapters, a variety of figures provide essential reference points for Jesus' adult ministry before John's first appearance in chapter 3: Abraham and David, Joseph and Mary, Herod and the magi, among others. In contrast, Mark's presentation of the context and starting point of Jesus' ministry is stark in its simplicity.

Mark opens with an announcement: "The beginning of the Gospel of Jesus Christ the Son of God."[9] As we read on, we learn that the beginning of the Gospel of Jesus Christ coincides with the fulfillment of scriptural prophecy: "As it is written in Isaiah the prophet . . ." Surprisingly, the individual who fulfills the prophecy that follows is not Jesus but John the Baptist:

> Behold, I send my messenger before your face, who will prepare your way. The voice of one crying in the wilderness, "Prepare the way of the Lord, make straight his paths."[10]

In fact this is a composite quotation in which elements of scriptural passages from Exodus, Malachi, and Isaiah are combined to highlight the theme of preparation (wording adopted by the evangelist is emphasized):

> And *behold, I send my messenger before your face*, so that he may guard you in the way and bring you into the land that I prepared for you.[11]

> *Behold, I send* forth *my messenger who will prepare* a *way before* my *face*, and suddenly the Lord whom you seek will enter his temple—the Messenger of the covenant for whom you long, behold, he is coming, says the LORD God Almighty. And who shall endure the day of his coming, and who shall stand at his appearing?[12]

9. Mark 1:1.
10. Mark 1:2–3.
11. Exod. 23:20.
12. Mal. 3:1–2a.

The voice of one crying in the wilderness, "Prepare the way of the
LORD, *make straight* the *paths* of our God. Every valley shall be filled,
and every mountain and hill brought low. The crooked [paths] will
be made straight, and the rough a level plain."[13]

In itself the first of these passages (from Exodus) has nothing to
do with John the Baptist. The people of Israel receive a promise of
angelic guidance and protection; the "messenger" here is an angel.
The second passage (from Malachi) is more directly relevant. At the
end of this short book, the promised messenger is identified with
Elijah, who was taken up to heaven in a fiery chariot and who is
shortly to return: "Behold, I will send you Elijah the prophet before
the great and manifest day of the LORD."[14] John's followers seem to
have identified him with this returning Elijah, and this identification
was taken over by the first Christians.[15] The "leather girdle around
his waist"[16] was also Elijah's trademark.[17] Yet for Christians, Malachi's messenger passage needed to be reworded to create space for
Jesus between the appearances of "Elijah" and God himself. Exodus
provided the necessary rewording. And so the words "Behold, I send
forth my messenger who will prepare a way before *my* face" become
"Behold, I send my messenger before *your* face, who will prepare *your*
way."[18] The Malachi passage is rewritten, with help from Exodus, so
that the saying is now addressed by God to Jesus.

A similar alteration is made to the Isaiah quotation that follows.
The voice in the wilderness calls its hearers to "prepare the way of
the Lord" and to "make straight the paths of our God." In Mark's
version it is "*his* paths" that are made straight. If the evangelist had
retained the reference to God, then "the Lord" and "God" would be
synonymous, and there would be no place for Jesus. But "the Lord"

13. Isa. 40:3–4.
14. Mal. 4:5.
15. Cf. Mark 9:11–13.
16. Mark 1:6.
17. 2 Kings 1:8.
18. Mark 1:2.

might also be taken to refer to Jesus. In that case, "his paths" would refer to Jesus' ministry, understood as a journey.

Mark introduces his complex scriptural quotation with the words "As it is written in Isaiah the prophet." Recognizing that not all of the quotation is from Isaiah, some early scribes changed this to "As it is written in the prophets." Yet for Mark it is the Isaiah passage that is most important here. Isaiah alone provides two crucial components that are immediately applied to John the Baptist, namely, the references to the wilderness and to the voice: "John came baptizing *in the wilderness* and *proclaiming* a baptism for forgiveness of sins."[19]

Why is John the Baptist presented as the fulfillment of Scripture, so that Mark opens not with Jesus but with John? John is an impressive figure, but he seems quite alien to Jesus. If the scriptural "way of the Lord" is the way of Jesus himself, it is not clear how John prepares it or enables others to do so. In this gospel Jesus does not inherit John's followers, nor does he continue John's practice of baptizing people. Unlike John, he does not clothe himself in camel hair or feed himself with locusts and wild honey; so far as we know, his appearance and diet are entirely normal. The two figures are utterly different from each other. According to the scriptural quotation, John's ministry is to prepare the way for Jesus. But how does he do so? Why does Mark trace "the beginning of the Gospel of Jesus Christ" back to the ministry of John?

John the Baptist is associated here with the wilderness or desert. Although the river Jordan flows through this desert, it is an inhospitable place. Human life can be sustained there only with difficulty. Yet people flock to the desert from the whole of Judea to hear John preach and to submit to his baptism; indeed, we are even told that John's hearers include the entire population of Jerusalem.[20] From the city to the desert: this is a journey from an environment constructed by humans to one in which traces of human activity are virtually absent. John's hearers make this journey in order to confess their

19. Mark 1:4.
20. Mark 1:5.

sins and to be forgiven, drawn by the voice calling them to prepare
the Lord's way. If immersion in the river Jordan is the means to forgiveness, the desert is the place where John's hearers become clear
about themselves, their past, and their need for repentance. Distanced
from the familiar course of things in the inhabited parts of Judea or
the city of Jerusalem, the desert represents the possibility of a new
perspective on ordinary, everyday life—a perspective that is also a
self-imposed verdict on its compromises, evasions, and failures. The
verdict on the self is severe because its context is a covenant relationship between these people and their God, in which the privilege of
divine favor is tied to an exacting divine demand. They are aware
that they fall far short of what is required of them. Concepts such
as sin, repentance, confession, and forgiveness are not new to them.
The voice in the wilderness recalls what is already known yet half-
forgotten or suppressed.

John the Baptist is the leader of a movement of prophetic renewal,
and the themes of this renewal movement are not themselves alien
to the gospel. John "proclaims a baptism of repentance for forgiveness of sins,"[21] and these key terms will be echoed by Jesus, who will
call his hearers to "repent and believe the gospel"[22] and declare the
forgiveness of sins.[23] John also announces the coming of a "Stronger
One" whose shoelaces he is unworthy to untie and whose baptism
will no longer be with water but with the Holy Spirit.[24] Yet this is a
prophecy of an indefinite future rather than an announcement about
the present. When, in the very next verse, Jesus arrives on the scene,
there is nothing to identify him with the figure predicted by John.
The Stronger One will bring an infinitely superior baptism in a divine element, yet Jesus subjects himself to John's baptism of water.
John is overawed at the prospect of meeting the Stronger One, yet he
baptizes Jesus as just another anonymous member of the crowd that
has responded to his call from the wilderness. Jesus remains silent.

21. Mark 1:4.
22. Mark 1:15.
23. Mark 2:5.
24. Mark 1:7–8.

He does not explain that, as the sinless Son of God, he has no need to repent and confess his sins as the crowds do. On the contrary, he is simply one of the crowd, differing from the others only in that they have come from Judea and Jerusalem while he is a northerner, from Nazareth in Galilee.[25]

It is only when this newly baptized person emerges from the water that the difference between him and the others becomes significant. He experiences something that they do not. They may be elated by the certainty of sins forgiven, but they do not see what he sees or hear what he hears: the heavens split open, the dove descends, and the heavenly voice acknowledges him as the beloved son.[26] This is his own private experience. We are told that "*he saw* the heavens opened and the Spirit descending upon him like a dove." John is unaware of this, and no doubt has turned his attention to the next in the long line of candidates for baptism. In any case, John now drops out of view. There is a passing reference to his arrest[27] and, later, an account of his execution,[28] but his ministry is now at an end. After the baptism of Jesus, John and the crowds who line up for baptism simply vanish; Jesus at last takes on his role as protagonist of the gospel narrative.[29]

Has John succeeded in his vocation, which was to prepare the way of the Lord and make his paths straight? How has he done so? Jesus' relationship to John the Baptist in Mark is apparently as tenuous as his relationship to Joseph and his ancestors in Matthew. Despite appearances, however, the relationship must be real and important in both cases. Unless the evangelists unthinkingly reproduce traditional material that conflicts with their real intentions, Mark's John must be as significant for his interpretation of Jesus as Matthew's Joseph is for his. Mark chooses to open his narrative by speaking of the one who prepared the way of the Lord and made his paths straight. The Lord whose way was prepared is Jesus, and he and John encounter

25. Mark 1:9.
26. Mark 1:10–11.
27. Mark 1:14.
28. Mark 6:14–29.
29. Mark 1:1.

each other only on the occasion when the one was baptized by the
other. It is in baptizing Jesus that John fulfills the role appointed for
him in the prophetic utterances.

The Inclusive Gospel

According to Mark, John announced a "baptism of repentance" that
had as its aim "the forgiveness of sins."[30] This repentance is a public
event, not just a private one, for people are described as "confessing
their sins" as they are being baptized.[31] That does not mean that every
individual sin had to be recalled and acknowledged, as in some later
practices of confession. When the prodigal son confesses, "Father, I
have sinned before heaven and before you,"[32] he does not go into detail.
Confession may also be made on behalf of the community. So Daniel
confesses that "*we* have sinned and done wrong, acted wickedly and
rebelled, turning aside from your commandments and ordinances."[33]
When Isaiah sees his vision of the enthroned Lord, he confesses that
"I am a man of unclean lips and I live among a people of unclean
lips."[34] Here both individual and communal dimensions of confession are present. Yet confession remains a humiliating act of public
self-exposure in which one passes a negative verdict on the whole of
one's past life. John's baptism requires confession, and Jesus subjects
himself to this baptism.

This is, of course, surprising. Why would Jesus confess his sins
and seek forgiveness? Elsewhere in the New Testament it is said of
Jesus that he was "tempted in every way as we are, yet without sin."[35]
That Jesus was sinless seems to have been taken for granted by the
first Christians. Matthew shows that he is aware of the problem when
he has John initially refuse to baptize Jesus: "I need to be baptized

30. Mark 1:4.
31. Mark 1:5.
32. Luke 15:21.
33. Dan. 9:5.
34. Isa. 6:5.
35. Heb. 4:15.

by you, and do you come to me?"[36] In contrast, Mark shows no such concern. For this evangelist, Jesus' baptism and the descent of the Spirit and divine voice that follow it are *the model and prototype for Christian initiation*, the event in which one becomes a Christian and a member of the Christian community. There is indeed no rending of the heavens, descending dove, or divine voice in regular Christian initiation; these features of Mark's narrative are intended to make Jesus' empowerment by the Holy Spirit vivid and comprehensible to the reader. But this empowerment by the Spirit takes place in close connection with Jesus' baptism. Baptism and the descent of the Spirit are not two separate events, with the first as the more or less accidental occasion for the second. They are the negative and positive sides of a single event, the one side oriented toward overcoming the past, the other toward opening up a new future not determined by that past. The single event that inaugurated Jesus' ministry is reenacted whenever anyone joins the Christian community.

This becomes clear when we read Paul alongside Mark. At the most basic level, baptism is an act of washing. According to Paul, writing to the Corinthians, "You were washed, you were sanctified, you were justified in the name of the Lord Jesus Christ and in the Spirit of our God."[37] Sin defiles and must be washed away like dirt from the body, but this is just a necessary preliminary to a new relationship with God through Christ: "You who were baptized into Christ have put on Christ."[38] "Put on" suggests that new clothing replaces the old that was put off in baptism, and this new clothing represents an identity determined now by Christ rather than by the discarded past. More precisely, this new identity involves a participation in Jesus' own relationship to the God who acknowledges him as his son and whom he acknowledges as his father. God

> sent forth his son, born of a woman, born under the law, so that we might be redeemed from the law, so that we might receive adoption

36. Matt. 3:14.
37. 1 Cor. 6:11.
38. Gal. 3:27.

as sons. And because you are sons, God sent forth the Spirit of his son into our hearts, crying *Abba* (Father).[39]

This Pauline passage is closely related to Mark's account of Jesus' baptism. The themes of sonship and the Spirit are present in both, with a particular focus on Jesus' experience of God. *Abba* is the Aramaic word Jesus uses to address God, and it is preserved by Paul alongside its Greek translation, *ho Patēr*, "[the] Father." This combination of the Aramaic term and its Greek equivalent also occurs in Mark's Gethsemane narrative: "*Abba* (Father), all things are possible to you; take this cup from me."[40] While *Abba* does not occur in Mark's baptism story, it is presupposed there; for if God acknowledges Jesus as God's beloved son, and if Jesus accepts the identity ascribed to him, then he must acknowledge God as *Abba*, his beloved father. In Mark as in Paul, the mutual recognition of parent and child occurs through the Spirit, who "descends" (Mark) or who is "sent forth" (Paul). This mutuality is made explicit in a passage from 2 Corinthians in which scriptural language is freely adapted and in which the addition of "daughters" to "sons" indicates that the new relationship established in baptism is fully inclusive: "I will be a father to you, and you will be sons and daughters to me, says the Lord Almighty."[41] As portrayed by Mark, Jesus' baptism is the prototype of precisely this relationship.

Jesus' baptism does not concern him alone. The new identity bestowed on him through the Spirit and the divine voice is open to participation by others. This baptism is an inclusive event, and Mark's Christian readers recognize in it their own experience of turning from the old life to the new. That is why his account of the ministry of John the Baptist can be presented as "the beginning of the *gospel* of Jesus Christ." The word "gospel" does not refer merely to a narrative account of Jesus' ministry. Gospel is *euaggelion*, good news, and news becomes "good" only from the standpoint of its recipients.

39. Gal. 4:4–6.
40. Mark 14:36.
41. 2 Cor. 6:18.

Just this point was already made by Origen, the great third-century Alexandrian theologian, in his multivolume but unfinished commentary on the Gospel of John. Noting that the text on which he is commenting is designated a "gospel" or *euaggelion*, Origen asks himself what this term implies. His carefully crafted definition is quite general in form. *Euaggelion* is "speech announcing events that, rightly and because of the benefits they bring, bring joy to the hearer when the announcement is received."[42] On this definition, the event of Jesus' baptism can only be the beginning of the *gospel* if the written announcement of this event gives joy to the hearer and reader because of the benefits it brings. It cannot be merely an item in Jesus' personal life story; it must be an *inclusive* event, open to reenactment so that others may benefit from it. According to Paul, "Christ died for us."[43] According to Mark, Jesus already acted "for us" in subjecting himself to John's baptism of repentance.

An End and a Beginning

In the composite scriptural quotation that introduces the reader to John the Baptist, reference is made to a "way": a path or road, perhaps also a journey with a specific beginning and end. The promised messenger will "prepare your way." The voice crying out in the wilderness appeals to its hearers to "prepare the way of the Lord" and to "make his paths straight." John himself prepares the way, and he also appeals to others to do so. In reality, the evangelist allows little time for any such preparation. When the newly baptized Jesus has embarked on his independent activity, the time of preparation is over.

What is "the way of the Lord"? Mark's Jesus is constantly on the move, journeying from one location to another with restless energy. It is John who initiates this movement. When Mark says that "Jesus came from Nazareth of Galilee *and* was baptized by John," he means that Jesus came from Nazareth *in order to be* baptized by John.

42. Origen, *Commentary on John* 1.27.
43. Rom. 5:8.

The proclamation of a baptism of repentance sets Jesus in motion, drawing him out of a settled existence in a small Galilean town and into the Judean wilderness. Returning to Galilee after John's arrest, Jesus appears on the shore of Galilee's "sea" (or lake) before arriving at the town of Capernaum and visiting its synagogue.[44] These locations—the lake and the town—recur as the narrative unfolds. Jesus' way takes the form of small-scale circular journeys that begin and end in Galilee by way of the Judean desert,[45] Capernaum by way of the other Galilean towns,[46] and the lakeshore by way of an unspecified mountain and house[47] or the country of the Gerasenes.[48] Other places visited by Jesus include Nazareth, Bethsaida, and, further north, Tyre.[49] A strangely circuitous route leads him from Tyre through Sidon to the Sea of Galilee via the Decapolis.[50] Jesus and his disciples are constantly in motion, yet there seems to be no goal in view. That changes at Caesarea Philippi, where, after Peter has confessed him as the Christ, Jesus announces his forthcoming suffering, rejection, death, and resurrection.[51] This sequence of events is to be the end and goal of his journeying along "the way of the Lord."

That these events will take place in Jerusalem is finally made explicit in the third of the passion predictions that Mark attributes to Jesus:

> They were on the way, going up to Jerusalem, and Jesus went before them. And they were astonished, and those who followed were afraid. And taking the Twelve aside again, he began to tell them what was about to happen to him: "Behold, we are going up to Jerusalem, and the Son of man will be handed over to the chief priests and scribes, and they will condemn him to death and hand him over to the gentiles.

44. Mark 1:14–21.
45. Mark 1:9–14.
46. Mark 1:21–2:1.
47. Mark 3:7–4:1.
48. Mark 4:35–5:21.
49. Mark 6:1, 45; 7:24.
50. Mark 7:31.
51. Mark 8:31.

And they will mock him and spit upon him and scourge him and kill him. And after three days he will rise."[52]

Now the circular journeys in and around Galilee give way to a linear journey with a definitive conclusion, from Caesarea Philippi in the north to Jerusalem in the south. The journey is an ascent. One goes *up* to Jerusalem; each of the short pilgrim-psalms of the Psalter is identified as a *šîr hamma'ălôt*, "a Song of Ascents."[53] Yet the journey Jesus announces does not sound like a pilgrimage, although (as it turns out) its ending will coincide with the Feast of Passover. Pilgrims anticipate an encounter with the holy, a restored and renewed relationship with the Deity. Jesus anticipates his own destruction. He takes the way to Jerusalem as a free agent, but when he arrives there he will be deprived of his freedom and become a passive object in the hands of others. The final stage of his "way," from Gethsemane to Golgotha, will be involuntary. Yet in choosing to go up to Jerusalem he freely embraces his own loss of freedom as willed by God. The way he takes is "not what I will but what you will."[54] It is because the end of his way is willed by God that he can be so certain of it; there is no thought here of outcomes that are merely probable. The God who wills the end is no inscrutable, impersonal Fate but can be addressed—precisely at the end—as "Abba [Father]," as if in response to the divine acknowledgment of "my beloved son" at the beginning.

This, then, is "the way of the Lord" that it is John the Baptist's role to "prepare." The way of the Lord is the journey that begins when news of John's baptism draws Jesus from Nazareth in Galilee to the Judean desert and the river Jordan. It is this same journey that ends in Jerusalem. While it is true that lesser, often circular journeys have also taken place, Mark's Jesus is continually in motion and never at rest. Individual journeys blend into a single process of journeying, which is at first seemingly random but finally proceeds in a straight line from north to south and with a clear perception of the outcome.

52. Mark 10:32–34.
53. Pss. 120–134.
54. Mark 14:36.

How does the end and goal of the journey relate to the beginning? Shortly before his arrival in Jerusalem, Jesus provides his own interpretation of his journey's end:

> The Son of man came not to be served but to serve, and to give his life as a ransom for many.[55]

The Son of man becomes the servant of the many by giving up his own future in order to secure theirs. The many are in need of a "ransom," liberation from a captivity that is otherwise without end and without hope. In Gethsemane Jesus himself becomes a captive.[56] In the darkness of Golgotha he gives expression to the captive's despair: "My God, my God, why have you forsaken me?"[57] In giving up *himself* as a ransom for many, he enters their situation and makes it his own. His service to them is an act of supreme solidarity. The same is true at the beginning of Jesus' way, when he submits to a baptism of repentance and receives the Holy Spirit and the assurance of sonship. This too takes place on behalf of the "many" in whom this experience of liberation will be reenacted. Initiated by John the Baptist, the beginning of the "way of the Lord" is the same as its end.

This proximity of the end to the beginning is confirmed by one final Markan reference to Jesus' journeying. Arriving at his tomb early on Easter morning, Jesus' female disciples are instructed to pass on a message to their male colleagues: "Go, tell his disciples and Peter that he goes before you to Galilee. There you will see him."[58] The message is not passed on, for the women flee in terror from the tomb and say nothing.[59] Yet the announcement of the risen Lord's return to Galilee and the promise of a reunion still stand. In going before his followers to Galilee, he returns to the place from which he set out in the beginning, when he came from Nazareth in Galilee to be

55. Mark 10:45.
56. Mark 14:43–50.
57. Mark 15:34.
58. Mark 16:7.
59. Mark 16:8.

baptized by John in the Jordan. The linear movement that seemed to reach its conclusion in Jerusalem has become a circle.

If the end of the story brings us back to the beginning, then the story must be retold with the risen Lord as its protagonist. The retold story remains exactly as it was before, except that it now speaks of a figure contemporary with Mark and his readers, not one whose existence is confined to an ever-receding past.[60] It has become *gospel*, "speech announcing events that, rightly and because of the benefits they bring, bring joy to the hearer when the announcement is received." The evangelist might have anticipated the later convention that the gospel story should conclude with appearances of the risen Lord, whether in Galilee or Jerusalem or both. This later tradition is so familiar that the absence of appearance stories in Mark seems hard to understand. Yet the absence has its own positive significance, for it brings the reader back to the beginning, in Galilee, from where Jesus set out for the wilderness in order to be baptized by John in the river Jordan.

---

60. As Karl Barth puts it: "How can that which God did in Jesus Christ yesterday not be his act today and tomorrow?" (*CD* IV/2, 111).

3

The Third Gospel: Magnificat

The third of the canonical gospels did not begin life as the work of "Luke," nor does it identify itself as a "gospel." In a short but eloquent preface, the author names his dedicatee, Theophilus, but he does not give his own name. He selects the neutral term "narrative" (*diēgēsis*) to describe the kind of text this is, rather than following Mark's use of "gospel." The author knows of "many" such narratives but suggests that his is superior because it has been carefully researched; presumably this is not the case with the others. Its readers may therefore have absolute confidence in its reliability. All that and more is conveyed in a single long sentence:

> Since many others have attempted to compose a narrative of the events that have taken place among us, as communicated to us by the original eyewitnesses and servants of the word, it seemed appropriate for me also, after devoting long and careful study to the subject, to write for you a well-ordered account, most excellent Theophilus, so that you

may have reliable knowledge of the matters in which you have been instructed.[1]

The author is familiar with Mark (certainly) and Matthew (probably), but it is not his aim to establish his own work as a third gospel alongside the earlier two. He is more ambitious than that. While others have written an account of "the events that have taken place among us," his is to be the definitive version. It is hinted that the publication of this text makes earlier versions of the gospel story redundant, at least in principle. The work's dedicatee, the "most excellent Theophilus," also represents the ideal reader that the author imagines as he writes: one who finds in the new work the full, satisfying, and convincing account of the truth that has never been available before.

Ideal readers as imagined by an author do not normally coincide with real readers, who always have their own independent interests and agendas. In the course of the second century, at least four influential approaches to Luke came into being. None of these could have been foreseen by the evangelist himself.

How Luke Became Luke

The second-century reader who came closest to accepting Luke's definitive status was Marcion, who held the controversial view that the God revealed in Jesus Christ was other than and superior to the God of Jewish Scripture—a God of kindness and grace as opposed to a God of punitive justice. Marcion's gospel was an abbreviated version of Luke's, but for his many followers this gospel was neither Marcion's nor Luke's but simply "the Gospel" in its pure apostolic form. This abridged gospel lacked the authorial introduction, birth stories, and indeed almost everything else until the statement in Luke 4:31 that Jesus "came down to Capernaum, a city of Galilee." For Marcion, Jesus here takes human form as he descends directly from heaven. He derives nothing from a human parent, however, and he is entirely

1. Luke 1:1–4.

independent of Jewish Scripture. Thus scriptural references are elimi-
nated. For example, Luke has Jesus say, "This is an evil generation—it
seeks a sign, but no sign shall be given it except the sign of Jonah."[2]
Like the prophet Jonah, Jesus preaches a message of repentance. But
from Marcion's standpoint the two have nothing in common; they
are servants of different deities. He therefore eliminates the reference
to Jonah: "This generation, no sign shall be given it."[3] Yet it is only
Marcion's opponents who think of his gospel as a truncated and ano-
nymized version of Luke's. If Marcionite Christians came across the
Gospel of Luke, they would view its opening chapters and scriptural
references as spurious additions introduced by those who confused
the God of grace with the harsh retributive deity of Jewish Scripture.

For other second-century readers, Luke's birth stories and scriptural references were an asset rather than a problem. Yet Luke could
be valued not as an independent gospel in its own right but as a
supplement to Matthew, enhancing a narrative that is still primarily
Matthean. That is the case for Justin Martyr, a younger contemporary
of Marcion, and like him active in Rome. Justin's most substantial
surviving work is his *Dialogue with Trypho*, a partially or entirely
fictional account of a debate with a well-informed Jewish dialogue
partner about the Christian interpretation of Scripture. In the course
of a long and not very successful attempt to prove that Scripture foresaw the circumstances of Jesus' birth, Justin provides a summary of
the birth story in its Matthean form: Mary's pregnancy, the angelic
reassurance to Joseph, Herod and the magi, the flight to Egypt, and
the massacre of the innocents are all mentioned.[4] But Justin is aware
that Matthew does not tell the whole story, and he supplements his
summary with references to Luke's version (italicized):

> Joseph was commanded in a vision not to put away his wife; the angel
> who appeared to him told him that what was in her womb was of the

2. Luke 11:29.
3. The Marcionite gospel text can be partially reconstructed on the basis of evidence provided by Tertullian and Epiphanius.
4. Matt. 1–2.

Holy Spirit. Then he was afraid, and did not put her away; *but on the occasion of the first census which was taken in Judea, under Cyrenius, he went up from Nazareth where he lived, to Bethlehem to which he belonged, to be enrolled; for his family was of the tribe of Judah which then inhabited that region.* Then together with Mary he was commanded to journey to Egypt and to stay there with the child until another revelation instructed them to return to Judea. *But when the child was born in Bethlehem, since Joseph could not find a lodging in that village, he found shelter in a cave near the village. And while they were there, Mary gave birth to the Christ and placed him in a manger*, and here the magi who came from Arabia found him. . . . So Herod (when the magi from Arabia did not return to him as he had requested but had returned to their own country by another way, as they were told; and when Joseph, with Mary and the child, had now gone to Egypt, as it was revealed to them that they should do), as he did not know which child the magi had gone to worship, ordered that all the children in Bethlehem should be massacred.[5]

Justin has some difficulty putting these events into a coherent sequence, but his attitude toward the two gospel birth stories is clear. Matthew provides the basic account, which Justin summarizes in some detail. Luke is used more selectively; Justin draws from Luke his references to the accommodation problem and the manger, but the child in the manger is visited not by Luke's shepherds but by Matthew's magi. The manger is located in a cave, not a stable. Both traditional locations attempt to fill a gap in Luke's narrative, which says only that Mary laid her child in a manger because there was no room for them in the inn.[6] Justin thinks well of Luke, but for him the definitive gospel is still Matthew's.

Justin presents himself as a teacher of philosophy—a Christian teacher of the Christian philosophy, who provides his students with the intellectual equipment needed to defend the truth of the Christian message against its educated critics. His best-known student,

5. Justin Martyr, *Dialogue with Trypho* 78.3–7. Cf. Luke 2:2, 4–5, 7.
6. Luke 2:7.

Tatian, produced a comprehensive gospel text drawn from all four canonical gospels with additional details from other gospel texts or traditions. This work was available in both Greek and Syriac versions, both probably prepared by Tatian himself. It later came to be known as the *Diatessaron*, but in many Syriac-speaking churches it was simply "the Gospel," and the four individual gospels were barely known.[7] Only when it fell out of favor in the early fifth century was it finally supplanted by the "Gospel of the Separated," that is, by the individual gospels of the separate evangelists.[8]

Tatian's gospel or gospel edition began with the opening verses of John before switching to Luke for the account of the birth of John the Baptist. The original wording of the earlier gospels was adjusted at a number of points; Tatian's whole project assumed that existing gospels were unsatisfactory in their separated form, and he did not consider their texts to be sacrosanct. His own text is difficult to reconstruct in detail, but it seems to have opened roughly as follows. (Asterisks represent differences from John or Luke, whether alterations or omissions.)

> In the beginning was the Word, and the Word was with God, and the Word was God. He was in the beginning with God. All things were by him, and without him was not one thing. And that-which-exists *is by him, and *he is life, and the life is the light of men. The light *was shining in the darkness, and the darkness did not overcome it. In the days of Herod king of Judea there was a certain priest, and his name was Zechariah* and his wife was *Elisabeth. And they were both righteous before God, blameless *throughout their lives. But they had no child, because Elisabeth was barren and both were advanced in years. Now while he was serving in the order of the priesthood before

---

7. For the argument that the *Diatessaron* is better viewed as a gospel rather than a gospel harmony, see M. Crawford, "Diatessaron, a Misnomer?"

8. In the following discussion, I draw on my forthcoming article "Towards a Redaction-Critical Reading of the Diatessaron Gospel." The title *Evangelion da-Mepharreshe* ("Gospel of the Separated") occurs in the superscription of the two Old Syriac gospel manuscripts (the Sinaitic and the Curetonian) and in the subscription of the first of these. See F. C. Burkitt, ed., *Evangelion da-Mepharreshe*, 1:2, 534.

God, according to the custom of the *division of the priesthood, it
fell to him to offer incense.[9]

In the passage from Luke, Tatian seems to have omitted details
that draw attention to the narrative's Jewish context. Luke says that
Zechariah and Elisabeth "walked in all the commandments and ordinances of the Lord, blameless." Tatian replaces this reference to the
law of Moses with the statement that they were "blameless throughout their lives." But the most profound change is that the difference
between John and Luke is erased. If Tatian was familiar with the
traditional evangelist names, he did not pass them on to users of his
own work—nor did he attach his own name to it. Points of transi-
tion from one gospel to another are not identified, for the intention
is precisely to eliminate gospel differences and to blend all available
material into a single comprehensive account. Unsurprisingly, Luke's
preface to his work is omitted.[10] Its assertion of individual authorship and its claim to superiority over rival texts have no place here.
Tatian treats Luke rather as Matthew treats Mark—as a source that
needs to be edited and integrated into a greater whole.

Luke's ideal reader is one who agrees with his own self-assessment:
his carefully researched work gives a more trustworthy account of
the Lord's words and deeds than any of its predecessors. Perhaps the
most excellent Theophilus was persuaded by this; Marcion, Justin,
and Tatian were not. Neither was Irenaeus, bishop of Lyons, who did
more than anyone to establish the four-gospel collection. Luke has his
place in this collection, but it is not a privileged place. On the other
hand, Irenaeus does respect and preserve his individuality, providing
the anonymous evangelist with his familiar name, "Luke," and his
heavenly symbol, the calf. Irenaeus may draw from earlier tradition

9. Tentative reconstructions of the diatessaronic text may be carried out with
the help of Latin and Arabic translations (from which, however, many distinctive
features have been removed) and the *Commentary* by Ephrem, a fourth-century
Syriac-speaking theologian. Supporting evidence is sometimes found in the Old
Syriac gospel translation.

10. Luke 1:1–4.

in either or both of these cases, but these are the earliest examples of the name and the symbol in the surviving literature.

Why was the Third Evangelist identified as "Luke"? Other traditional evangelist names refer to known individuals. Matthew is identified with "Matthew the tax collector," who is paired with the apostle Thomas in the first gospel's listing of the twelve apostles.[11] The reference to Matthew's occupation directs the reader back to the occasion when Jesus calls a tax collector by the name of Matthew to be his disciple.[12] Matthew's name replaces that of Levi in the equivalent passage in Mark,[13] and the traditional evangelist name may be a deduction from the double reference to Matthew within the Matthean text. If so, it is hardly an obvious deduction, and it lacks historical credibility. In the case of Luke, alert early readers will have found rather more clues to authorial identity. The author identifies himself as one familiar with the apostolic testimony but not himself an apostle.[14] In Acts, his second volume, he speaks from time to time in the first person plural, suggesting that he was once a companion of the apostle Paul. In the course of Paul's so-called second missionary journey, we read that *they* came to Troas" but that, after divine guidance through a dream, "*we* decided to go to Macedonia."[15] At the end of the Acts narrative, the author describes what happened "when *we* entered Rome."[16] If the evangelist was a companion of Paul, it might seem reasonable to suppose that his gospel must have derived from Paul's preaching, just as Mark's was supposedly based on Peter's preaching. Who, then, was this third evangelist? Here Irenaeus (or some unknown predecessor) seems to have made an acute observation. As Paul awaits his death in a Roman prison, he reports that his fellow workers have left him to pursue their labors elsewhere—all but one of them: "Luke alone is

11. Matt. 10:3.
12. Matt. 9:9.
13. Mark 2:14.
14. Luke 1:2.
15. Acts 16:8–10.
16. Acts 28:16.

with me."[17] Elsewhere this same Luke is referred to as "the beloved physician."[18] Does Paul need to keep Luke by his side for medical reasons? Whatever the reason, Luke is uniquely placed to familiarize himself with Paul's testimony and to preserve it for posterity by putting it into writing. And so, according to Irenaeus, the evangelist should be identified as Luke, and his gospel should be seen as enshrining the testimony of Paul.[19] This third evangelist worked in close parallel with the second. After the deaths of Peter and Paul,

> Mark, the disciple and interpreter of Peter, handed down to us in written form what was preached by Peter, and Luke, the follower of Paul, set down in a book the gospel preached by him.[20]

This identification of the Third Evangelist with Luke the beloved physician is arguably quite plausible, if those first-person-plural passages in Acts are genuinely autobiographical. Yet the evangelists' names represent more than just conjectures about authorial identities; their most important role is to *differentiate* and *individualize* the texts to which they are attached. That is why evangelists' names still appear on just about every page of every book about the gospels. To name Luke as Luke is to assert that there is a place for distinctiveness within the fourfold canonical gospel, and that this distinctiveness is to be found throughout the text that bears his name, even in material shared with other evangelists. Multiple versions of the same material are not interchangeable, nor are they redundant. Even where differences of wording are minimal (as is sometimes though not often the case), differences of immediate or overall context remain. Collectively, the names underline the indirect, mediated character of the fourfold gospel's testimony to Jesus. This gospel is never just gospel; it is always the *gospel according to . . .* , one of a number of

17. 2 Tim. 4:11.

18. Col. 4:14; cf. Philem. 23.

19. Cf. D. Trobisch, *First Edition of the New Testament*, 45–55. Trobisch argues that the names of Luke and the other evangelists were deductions from the New Testament texts.

20. Irenaeus, *Against Heresies* 3.1.1.

interpretations of what has taken place in Jesus rather than a pure transcript that gives direct and exclusive access to its object. To put the point another way, the Jesus of these texts is never just Jesus, Jesus as he was in himself. He is always accompanied by an evangelist who serves as his interpreter, communicating his significance from within that evangelist's own distinctive perspective.

Historically, it is only as "Luke" that the text to which this name was attached has preserved the individuality and integrity asserted in its opening verses. The name proved necessary for its survival— although not as the definitive text its author may have wished it to be, but as one of just four instances of that strange new genre, that of the *gospel according to . . .*

Reassuring Theophilus

Luke continues to assert his individuality throughout his two long opening chapters. Only with his account of John the Baptist's ministry in chapter 3 does his narrative begin to run in parallel to Mark and Matthew, and even here there are a number of distinctive features. John's ministry is impressively introduced with references to secular rulers both well known (Tiberius, Pontius Pilate, Herod Agrippa) and obscure (Philip, Lysanias), to leading clerics (Annas, Caiaphas), and to territories that will feature in Luke's narrative (Judea, Galilee) and those that will not (Iturea, Trachonitis, Abilene). Several of these persons or locations were no doubt as obscure to Luke's first readers as they are to his present-day ones. But that is part of the intended effect of Luke 3:1–2: to summon up a broad historical, cultural, and geographical context that will enhance the significance of the moment when "the word of God came to John son of Zechariah in the desert."[21]

The timing of this event is also carefully noted. It took place "in the fifteenth year of the rule of Tiberius Caesar."[22] It is assumed that the reader has a fairly clear idea of the sequence of Roman

21. Luke 3:2.
22. Luke 3:1.

emperors from Augustus down to Luke's day, and that the fifteenth year of Tiberius has a meaningful place on the mental time line. Having learned previously of Augustus's decree that all the world be taxed, issued while Quirinius was governor of Syria,[23] a well-informed reader such as Theophilus will be reassured that the gospel events unfold within historical rather than mythological time.

Theophilus needed that reassurance. Subtly, Luke's preface implies that his predecessors have failed to persuade better-educated readers of the truth of the gospel events. Take Matthew, for example. Matthew seems to place the ministry of John the Baptist in the period immediately following Joseph's removal of his family to Galilee:

> And being warned in a dream he set out for the regions of Galilee, and when he arrived there he settled in a town called Nazareth. . . . In those days John the Baptist appeared, preaching in the desert of Judea. . . . Then Jesus came from Galilee to the Jordan to be baptized by John.[24]

Was Jesus just a child when he was baptized? There is nothing else in the narrative to suggest this. While the average reader of Matthew will not even notice this extraordinarily loose time frame, that is not so with Theophilus and his peers, who know about accurate datings and why they matter. At this point Luke steps in with various items of chronological information. John's ministry occurs during the fifteenth year of the emperor Tiberius; Jesus was "about thirty" when he came for baptism,[25] and he must therefore have been born about fifteen years before the death of Augustus and the accession of Tiberius. Another chronological reference point occurs in Luke's story of the twelve-year-old Jesus remaining behind in Jerusalem.[26] Artfully, the temporal gap created when Matthew prefaces the ministry of John the Baptist with a birth story is filled up. Jesus' parents went up to Jerusalem *each year* to celebrate the Passover; Jesus

23. Luke 2:1–2.
24. Matt. 2:22–3:1, 13.
25. Luke 3:23.
26. Luke 2:41–51.

grew in wisdom and in stature.[27] In such indications the passing of time is noted.

Luke's attempt to provide the gospel events with a more precise chronological framework is one of the ways in which he fulfills his promise to his reader in his preface. What is promised is an orderly, coherent, and sequential account of the gospel events based on long and careful study. An orderly account will also be a credible account; a disordered narrative undermines its own credibility. Luke suggests that this orderliness is lacking in earlier accounts, among them Mark and Matthew, on whom he is dependent for much of the content of his own work—along with other unknown sources textual or oral. Luke's concept of an orderly narrative may be seen in his varied responses to what he finds in Mark and Matthew.

Each evangelist opens his work by setting Jesus' ministry within a broader context. For Mark, this context is simply the ministry of John the Baptist. For Matthew, three additional elements must be supplied in order to lay the firmest possible foundation for the story that is to be told. First, there is the Messiah's genealogy, which shows that he is the fulfillment of Israel's scriptural history.[28] Second, there is the annunciation (to Joseph) of Jesus' miraculous conception as Immanuel, God-with-us, concluding with a brief reference to his birth.[29] Third, there is a self-contained account of the epiphany to the magi and its tragic aftermath—the flight to Egypt, the massacre of the innocents, the move to Nazareth.[30] What comes first in Mark—the ministry of John the Baptist—is the fourth and final element in Matthew's attempt to place Jesus' ministry in an appropriate context.

All four of these Matthean elements are taken over and adapted by Luke: genealogy, annunciation, epiphany, baptism. We have already seen how Luke's introduction of John the Baptist responds to perceived inadequacies in the Matthean equivalent. In the preceding

27. Luke 2:41, 52.
28. Matt. 1:1–17.
29. Matt. 1:18–25.
30. Matt. 2:1–23.

material too, the later evangelist engages with Matthean themes in his own distinctive way.

Genealogy. Matthew's gospel opens with a carefully structured genealogy tracing Jesus' ancestry from Abraham through David, Solomon, and the kings of Judah. Luke responds with a genealogy of his own but relegates it from first to fourth place[31] so that it now follows his account of the ministry of John.[32] Whereas Matthew starts with Abraham, Luke works backward from Jesus himself. The line of descent from David is no longer through Solomon and the kings of Judah, so most of the names are different; and the lineage is extended beyond Abraham all the way back to Adam. Now the Messiah's birth is the culmination of the entire human story, not just the Jewish one—although the universal human story is still outlined in Jewish scriptural terms.

Annunciation. In Matthew, the genealogy is followed by a brief narrative that begins with Mary's pregnancy and ends with Jesus' birth and naming,[33] but that is chiefly concerned with an angelic annunciation to Joseph that enables him (and the reader) to view these events in their proper light. The narrative says nothing about the time or place of these events; Bethlehem and Nazareth are first mentioned only in Matthew's second chapter. No other contextual information is provided about Joseph or Mary, who almost seem to exist in a vacuum. Luke also takes up the annunciation theme but (1) divides it in two, so that John's birth as well as Jesus' is foretold; (2) makes Mary rather than Joseph the addressee of the announcement relating to Jesus; and (3) supplies the necessary chronological and contextual information. These events took place "in the days of Herod king of Judah" (an expression based on Matt. 2:1, where, however, it introduces the *third* element in the Matthean sequence). The main characters, Zechariah, Elisabeth, and Mary, are all carefully introduced.[34]

31. Luke 3:23–38.
32. Luke 3:1–22.
33. Matt. 1:18, 25.
34. Luke 1:5–7, 27.

Epiphany. Belatedly, Matthew tells us that the birth of Jesus took place in Bethlehem of Judea in the days of Herod the king.[35] This information is provided only to prepare for the story of the magi, in which Bethlehem and Herod the king are essential elements. While the term "epiphany" is traditionally associated with the magi, who are led by the star to worship the future messianic king, this theme is also present in Luke, in whose treatment it again divides and multiplies. Here it is shepherds who are led to the Christ-child by an angelic revelation, just as Simeon and Anna are enabled to recognize him on the occasion of his presentation in the temple.[36] For Luke the event of the birth itself deserves greater prominence than it receives in Matthew, where it is mentioned only briefly at the end of the Joseph-focused annunciation account[37] and at the beginning of the story of the magi.[38] Yet, in Luke as in Matthew, the birth event again marks the boundary between narratives of annunciation and epiphany that are relatively self-contained and independent of each other. Following the annunciations, a new start is therefore needed:

Matthew: And when Jesus was born in Bethlehem of Judea in the days of Herod the king . . .[39]

Luke: And it came to pass that in those days a decree went forth from Caesar Augustus that all the world should be enrolled. . . .[40]

It is precisely the parallels between the two narratives that produce the contrasts.

Reading in Parallel

In all these parallels and contrasts, does Luke really imply *criticism* of Matthew? Perhaps he intended to *complement* him, for example, in

35. Matt. 2:1.
36. Luke 2:8–20, 22–35.
37. Matt. 1:25.
38. Matt. 2:1.
39. Matt. 2:1.
40. Luke 2:1.

giving Mary rather than Joseph the leading role in the birth stories? A clear distinction must be drawn between the evangelist's intention and the interpretative principles required by the fourfold canonical gospel. On the one hand, the conflicting genealogies make it unlikely that Luke intended to complement Matthew. One does not complement a genealogy by producing an entirely different set of ancestors for the same individual. On the other hand, the presence of both gospels within the canonical collection obliges the interpreter to seek complementarity at the theological level, even at points where a literal-historical reading can find only tension. If the theological purpose of one genealogy is to emphasize Jesus' Jewishness, while the other highlights his significance for all humanity, that cannot so easily be dismissed as a contradiction.

How might the birth stories in Matthew and Luke be read as complementary to each other, each with a perspective on its subject matter—the beginnings of Jesus' life—that is theologically valid in itself but also in its relation to the other?[41] Matthew's birth story is dominated by suffering in various forms. Luke's is dominated by celebration, praise, and thanksgiving. Matthew's version anticipates the suffering that Jesus will undergo on the cross, where he will experience not only physical pain but also forsakenness by God.[42] Luke's version anticipates Jesus' resurrection and ascension; his gospel will close with the disciples in the temple offering unceasing praise to God.[43] In Matthew, Jesus' death on the cross already casts its shadow back onto his birth. In Luke, Easter joy is already anticipated in the songs of Mary, Zechariah, Simeon, and the angels. The distinctive character of Luke's narrative is especially clear when set against the backdrop of Matthew's.

In Matthew, Mary is "found to be pregnant."[44] Her pregnancy is "from the Holy Spirit," as the evangelist hastens to add, but Joseph is not yet aware of that fact. Mary herself is passive. She does not

41. The question is addressed by B. Childs, *New Testament as Canon*, 161–65, but underplayed by R. Brown, *Birth of the Messiah*.
42. Matt. 27:46.
43. Luke 24:53.
44. Matt. 1:18.

communicate the fact of her pregnancy and try to explain it. Indeed, she utters not a single word in this birth narrative. Neither does Joseph, but he is at least presented as a free agent. In Mary's case, even her name drops out in the course of chapter 2. The magi see the child "with Mary his mother,"[45] but angelic instructions refer simply to "the child and his mother."[46] It is left to the reader to imagine Mary's suffering at the accusation of unfaithfulness. It is said only that Joseph—whose mental anguish is again left to the imagination—was determined to minimize the public scandal by quietly breaking off the engagement.[47] Was the engagement not already public knowledge? Is Joseph's idea that she should now be freed to become engaged to her unknown lover? Although these misconceptions are laid to rest through an angelic revelation, the question of Mary's adultery has been raised, briefly but explicitly. The conception of the Christ is attended by the suffering and shaming of the mother and the surrogate father. Matthew does not explicitly draw attention to this. Everything in his narrative is strictly objective; nothing is said about the emotions of the two participants. Yet the painful realities of the situation are obvious to the reader.

In Luke these complexities have vanished. Joseph himself is absent until the visit to Bethlehem and the birth, and the male role passes to Zechariah, father of John the Baptist, who receives an annunciation of his own. Here Mary memorably affirms and accepts her own role: "Behold, the handmaiden of the Lord; let it be to me according to your word."[48] No character in this story so much as hints at adultery. Visiting Zechariah and Elisabeth, Mary finds the supportive community she needs in her unique situation. Even Elisabeth's unborn child acknowledges her as the mother of the Christ, leaping for joy in the womb, and Elisabeth herself acclaims her in ecstatic prophetic utterance.[49] Mary rejoices in God her savior and returns again to her home, a free agent

45. Matt. 2:11.
46. Matt. 2:13–14, 20–21.
47. Matt. 1:19.
48. Luke 1:38.
49. Luke 1:40–45.

who comes and goes as she pleases with no hint of fear or shame.[50] Meanwhile the child John is born to Elisabeth, and again there is joy and gladness: her neighbors and relatives "heard that the Lord had multiplied his mercy to her, and they rejoiced with her."[51] The chapter concludes with Zechariah blessing the Lord, filled with the Holy Spirit.[52]

The contrast with the prelude to Jesus' birth in Matthew could hardly be sharper. Yet the theme is the same: the miraculous conception of the child who is to exercise a unique and decisive role in God's dealings with God's people, embodying the fullness of the divine presence in the world. Luke's and Matthew's infancy narratives are not two separate stories but the same story told from different perspectives. The miracle is a sign that the human life it initiates is a divine *gift*, not simply to the parents and child themselves (as in any other conception), but to the world. As the Fourth Evangelist writes, "God so loved the world that he *gave* his only Son."[53] The event of the conception itself is not narrated; the same will later be true of the resurrection. At the beginning of the gospel story as at the end, the divine action remains veiled in mystery. The narratives focus instead on the angelic disclosure or annunciation of the divine action to Mary or Joseph at the beginning and to the women on Easter morning at the end. There is symmetry and harmony in these angelic announcements at the beginning and end of the parallel narratives:[54]

> *Matthew*: As he considered these matters, behold, an angel of the Lord appeared to him in a dream, saying, "Joseph son of David, do not be afraid to take Mary as your wife. For what is conceived in her is from the Holy Spirit. She will bear a son, and you shall call his name Jesus, for he will save his people from their sins."[55]

50. Luke 1:47, 56.
51. Luke 1:58.
52. Luke 1:67–68.
53. John 3:16.
54. A point developed at length by Karl Barth, *CD* III/3, 499–511.
55. Matt. 1:20–21.

Luke: And the angel said to her, "Do not be afraid, Mary, for you have found favor with God. And behold, you will conceive in your womb and you will bear a son, and you shall call his name Jesus, for he will be great and will be called the Son of the Most High."[56]

Matthew: And the angel said to the women, "Do not be afraid, for I know that you seek Jesus the crucified. He is not here, he has been raised, as he said; come, see the place where he was laid."[57]

Luke: And behold, two men stood by them in shining garments. As they were afraid and prostrated themselves on the ground, they said to them, "Why do you seek the living among the dead? He is not here, he has been raised."[58]

At the beginning as at the end, the two evangelists tell the same story differently. Both points—sameness and difference—must be emphasized equally. Without sameness or oneness there would be no singular *gospel according to . . .* , but a chaos of incompatible versions of the "good news." Without difference there would not be four gospels but one. For that reason, Matthew's and Luke's accounts of the same event *must* differ.

Joy is not absent from Matthew's birth narrative. The magi "rejoice with very great joy" when the guiding star comes to a halt above the place where the child is.[59] Yet their visit brings no joy to anyone else. Joseph, Mary, and the child flee for their lives, the children of Bethlehem are slaughtered, and their mothers grieve inconsolably. Matthew's account of the sequel to Jesus' birth is perhaps the most distressing story in the entire Bible. Here the narrative is no longer restricted to objective facts, as words uttered long before by the prophet Jeremiah find a new application:

56. Luke 1:30–32.
57. Matt. 28:5–6.
58. Luke 24:4–5.
59. Matt. 2:10.

A voice was heard in Ramah, weeping and great mourning, Rachel weeping for her children. And she refused to be comforted, for they were not.[60]

Rachel, wife of Jacob and mother of Joseph and Benjamin, was buried in Bethlehem,[61] and she it is who gives voice to the town's bereaved inhabitants. Here too there is symmetry between the beginning and end of the story. At the end there is another cry of passionate grief:

And from the sixth hour there was darkness over all the land until the ninth hour. And at about the ninth hour Jesus cried out with a loud voice, "*Eli, Eli, lema sabachthani*," that is, "My God, my God, why have you forsaken me?"[62]

The darkness at Golgotha has already overshadowed Bethlehem. While the Christ-child and his parents escaped the massacre there, the crucified Jesus finally expresses his solidarity with its victims.

The end of the story is not only darkness; it is also the light of Luke's radiant angels on Easter morning. The beginning too must be light, and not only darkness. In Matthew, the light that shines in the darkness is the guiding star; in Luke, the light is the glory of the Lord that shines upon the shepherds keeping watch over their flocks by night.[63] The initial reaction to the heavenly light is fear, and those on whom it shines must be told, "Fear not." The light is the light of revelation, suddenly breaking into the world from above and transforming it. The revelation to the shepherds tells of "a great joy which shall be to all the people," the joy of the coming Savior, who is Christ the Lord.[64] The revelation immediately evokes praise, not as yet from the shepherds, but from the accompanying angels, who sing, "Glory to God in the heights, and on earth peace."[65] The shepherds

60. Matt. 2:18, citing Jer. 31:15. On this see R. Hays, *Reading Backwards*, 41–43.
61. Gen. 35:19–20.
62. Matt. 27:45–46; cf. Mark 15:33–34.
63. Luke 2:9.
64. Luke 2:10–11.
65. Luke 2:14.

will later take up the song as they return from Bethlehem "glorifying and praising God for all they had heard and seen."[66]

At one point Luke's celebrated and much-loved account of Jesus' birth is interrupted. The events of that night follow one another in their familiar sequence, but for a moment we are taken out of their time frame so as to look back on them and reflect on their meaning:

> And all who heard were amazed at what was told them by the shepherds. *(But Mary treasured all these words and pondered them in her heart.)* And the shepherds departed, glorifying and praising God.[67]

Mary here replaces Theophilus in the role of Luke's ideal reader. She "treasures all these words," which are also Luke's words, the words of his text. This text does not instantly yield up its meaning and significance, allowing its readers to assimilate what it teaches and to move on to something else. With Mary, they are to treasure it and meditate on it. If Mary's reflection on the words stored up in this text is an example to the reader, then so too is her song of praise: "My soul magnifies the Lord, and my spirit rejoices in God my Savior."[68] Here too the time frame of the narrative is temporarily suspended. Within the narrative Mary plays a central role. She is rightly acclaimed by Elisabeth as "the mother of my Lord,"[69] a scriptural precedent for the still more exalted title later bestowed on her: *Theotokos*, Mother of God. Yet the evangelist can also cause her to stand outside the narrative, looking in on it alongside the reader and leading meditation into praise.

66. Luke 2:20.
67. Luke 2:18–20; cf. 2:51.
68. Luke 1:46–47.
69. Luke 1:43.

4

The Fourth Gospel: Seeing God

Toward the end of his letter to the Galatians, the apostle Paul exhorts his readers to "do good to all, especially to those who are of the household of faith."[1] More than three hundred years later, Jerome writes a commentary on Galatians, reaches this verse, and is reminded of a legend he has heard about the final days in the life of the apostle John. The legend is only loosely related to the Galatians passage, but it is a good story and Jerome decides to include it anyway:

> The blessed evangelist John remained in Ephesus until extreme old age, when he could scarcely be carried to church anymore in his disciples' arms. When he was no longer able to utter many words, he used to say no more than "Children, love one another" at each of their assemblies. In the end the assembled disciples and brethren grew tired of always hearing the same thing, and they said, "Master, why do you

1. Gal. 6:10.

always say that?" John replied with the worthy statement, "Because it is the Lord's commandment, and if that alone is done, it suffices."[2]

The legend grew out of the Johannine account of Jesus washing his disciples' feet, a symbolic action whose significance is summed up in a "new commandment." Addressing his disciples as "children," Jesus says,

> A new commandment I give you, that you love one another—just as I have loved you, that you love one another. By this all will know that you are my disciples, if you have love for one another.[3]

In the legend, the aged John has taken this new commandment to heart. It is always "new" because it is always applicable in each new situation, so it cannot be repeated too often. John is well positioned to pass on this teaching. Already in the time of Irenaeus, John was identified with the anonymous "disciple whom Jesus loved," who "reclined at Jesus' breast" at the Last Supper.[4] John, the beloved disciple, understands that the relationship between Jesus and his own is a relationship of love, and that those who know themselves to be loved will extend that love to others. The aged John recalls the teaching he received, long ago, at the breast of Jesus.

The legend assumes that "the blessed evangelist John" has already written his gospel. Although nothing is said here about why or when it was composed, the legend's focus on John's "extreme old age" echoes the tradition that he was already old when he wrote it. As he repeats the Lord's new commandment again and again, John also summarizes the content of his gospel. For the legend, the Gospel of John is the gospel of love: "God so loved the world . . . ," that is, "God loved the world *in this way*, that he gave his only Son . . ."[5] If John's disciples at Ephesus practice the love of which he speaks, they

2. Jerome, *Commentary on Galatians* (on Gal. 6:10).
3. John 13:34–35.
4. John 13:23, 25; 21:20.
5. John 3:16.

will have understood the heart of his gospel—interpreting it truly, though indirectly, in their daily conduct.

Why was John supposed to have written his gospel when he was already an old man? This tradition too may be traced back to Irenaeus's account of gospel origins. Matthew is said to have written his gospel while Peter and Paul were preaching in Rome, whereas Mark and Luke wrote after the deaths of Peter and Paul. A distinction is made here between an apostolic age, during which Matthew writes and Peter and Paul preach, and a postapostolic age in which these apostles' teaching is preserved by their followers. But there is at least one apostle who survives well into this postapostolic age. After the Gospel of Matthew was followed by the postapostolic Gospels of Mark and Luke, "John the disciple of the Lord, who reclined on his breast, published a gospel while living in Ephesus in Asia."[6] This second apostolic gospel is strangely belated. Irenaeus believed that John's lifetime extended into the reign of the emperor Trajan (98–117 CE).[7] Even if John son of Zebedee was about twenty years old when a thirty-year-old Jesus called him and his brother away from their fishing, he would still have been at least ninety when he died. If John was similar in age to Jesus, then he could have lived until he was well over one hundred years old. When the later legend depicts a figure so weak that he can hardly even be carried to church, that is the age range it has in view.

As we saw in the last chapter, Irenaeus may himself have been responsible for identifying the anonymous author of the gospel for Theophilus as "Luke the beloved physician," said to have been Paul's only companion during the final days of his life. Irenaeus may also have been responsible for identifying the anonymous Fourth Evangelist as the apostle John. The oldest surviving references to Luke and John as evangelists occur in Irenaeus's work, although in both cases these identifications are based on earlier evidence. Whether or not either is correct, they have not simply been invented. In the case

6. Irenaeus, *Against Heresies* 3.1.1.
7. Irenaeus, *Against Heresies* 3.3.4.

of John, Irenaeus seems to have found the evidence he needed in the
five-volume *Exposition of the Lord's Sayings*, composed in the 120s
or 130s by Papias, bishop of Hierapolis.

Although this work has been lost, excerpts from its preface are
preserved in Eusebius's great *Church History*. In this preface Papias
names the first two evangelists as Matthew and Mark, and he is the
first to do so. He also refers twice to an individual named John. The
first reference is to John the son of Zebedee, occurring in a list in
which seven of the original twelve disciples are named. All of these
seem to be figures of the past, as one would expect if Papias is writing in the early second century. He claims to have collected reports
of their teaching from older contemporaries who knew them, but he
says nothing about a written gospel linked with John. On the contrary, Papias prefers "the living and abiding voice" of oral tradition
to "what is drawn from books." But he also claims to have received
reports of two other figures who are still teaching in his own day.
One of these is an unknown Aristion; the other is "the Elder John."
He writes as follows:

> If anyone came who had been a follower of the elders, I inquired
> about the words of the elders—what Andrew or what Peter said, or
> Philip or Thomas or James or John or Matthew, or any other of the
> Lord's disciples; and what Aristion and the Elder John, the Lord's
> disciples, say.[8]

Who is this second John, apparently distinguished from the first,
although both are numbered among the elders and the Lord's disciples? Irenaeus believed that they were one and the same. He was
familiar with the so-called Second Epistle of John, whose author
introduces himself anonymously as "the Elder."[9] On stylistic grounds
it seemed possible to identify the author of the Johannine Epistles
with the Fourth Evangelist. So, if Papias's "Elder John" was both the
apostle John and "the Elder" of 2 John, then the evangelist was the

8. Cited in Eusebius, *Church History* 3.39.4.
9. 2 John 1.

apostle John. In that way, the gospel of the beloved disciple becomes the Gospel according to *John*. Irenaeus presumably thought that Papias wrote during the reign of Trajan, in the first two decades of the second century; if John (the apostle John) was still alive then, he must have been immensely long-lived. By fusing into one the lives of Papias's two John figures, Irenaeus bestows extreme longevity on the apostle, who also becomes an evangelist. That is how an apostolic fourth gospel can come *after* a "postapostolic" second and third. For Irenaeus, the advantage of this long-lived evangelist is that the gap between his own day and the last surviving apostle is diminished. This makes it possible for him to claim that leading churchmen of the relatively recent past—Papias of Hierapolis, Polycarp of Smyrna—had firsthand knowledge of the elderly apostle during their youth. Justified skepticism about such claims was already expressed by Eusebius.[10]

Three plus One

The Gospel of John is often still described as "the fourth gospel" in modern scholarly writing. This expression came into vogue partly because of growing skepticism about the authorship of John son of Zebedee, but also because this gospel was still believed to have been written after the other three. It is typically dated to around 100 CE, whereas Matthew and Luke are dated to a decade or so earlier (ca. 85 CE) and Mark to a decade before that (ca. 75 CE). In truth, these conventional datings are impossible to verify; they are little more than informed guesses. If Luke was familiar with Matthew's gospel, some years would have elapsed between the composition of the two texts. The modern dating of John's gospel seems to be unconsciously influenced by Irenaeus's claim that it was written last, by a single individual who was still alive during the reign of the emperor Trajan. This dating overlooks the indications that this gospel took shape only gradually, over an extended period, and that it is the work

10. Eusebius, *Church History* 3.39.5–7.

not of a single author but of a "Johannine school." This text *may* have been the latest of the canonical four to have reached something like its present form, but that is not certain. The latest gospel could equally well have been Luke.

In spite of these uncertainties, it is appropriate to regard Luke as the third gospel in view of its close relationship to the earlier two. In contrast, John is the fourth gospel because of its difference from the other three. While it is true that all four gospels are distinctive and tell the same story in different ways, the distance separating John from the others is considerable. Over against this text, Matthew, Mark, and Luke form a coherent group of "synoptic" gospels. The fourfold gospel has a three-plus-one structure, as the following examples will demonstrate.

In John, the "cleansing of the temple" takes place at the beginning of Jesus' ministry and follows an incident—water turned to wine at Cana of Galilee—that is not recorded elsewhere.[11] In the synoptics, the temple incident takes place at the end of Jesus' ministry and is a link in the chain of events that leads to his death.

In John, most of Jesus' activity takes place in or around Jerusalem, which he visits for feasts such as Passover or Tabernacles on four occasions before the final Passover when he meets his death.[12] References to Jesus in Galilee are limited to three passages.[13] In the synoptics, Jesus' main activity takes place in or around Galilee, and he visits Jerusalem only once.

In John, Jesus' debates with opponents in Jerusalem focus mainly on the issue of who he claims to be. Even when he heals on the Sabbath, it is his identity that becomes the primary issue rather than Sabbath healing as such; the Jerusalem authorities seek to kill him because "he not only broke the Sabbath but also called God his own father, making himself equal to God."[14] In the synoptics, Jesus' debates occur in Galilee as well as Jerusalem, and they are mainly concerned with the observance and interpretation of the law.

11. John 2:1–11, 13–22.
12. John 2:13–4:3; 5:1–47; 7:1–10:21; 10:22–42.
13. John 2:1–12; 4:43–54; 6:1–7:9.
14. John 5:18.

In John, the event that leads to Jesus' death is the raising of Lazarus.[15] In the opinion of Caiaphas the high priest, this miracle poses a threat to public order with potentially disastrous consequences; the only responsible course is to put Jesus to death.[16] In the synoptics, Jesus performs no miracles in Jerusalem or its vicinity (apart from blighting a fig tree and restoring a severed ear). His death is unrelated to his activities as a miracle worker.

In John, Jesus speaks at length with his disciples about a future in which he will be absent and yet present to them in a new way, through the Paraclete, or Holy Spirit.[17] In the synoptics, this period of absence is viewed as a time of tribulation for the world that will culminate in the coming of the Son of man on the clouds of heaven.[18]

In John, Jesus prays for himself, his disciples, and future believers while still in the upper room following the Last Supper. Confident of his own destiny, he asks to be restored to the glory that he shared with his Father "before the foundation of the world."[19] In the synoptics, he is distressed at his forthcoming suffering and prays in Gethsemane that the cup of suffering be removed, while subjecting himself to his Father's will.

In John, Jesus' "glory" is manifested not only in his miracles but also and above all in his death. In death he is "exalted" or "glorified."[20] The cross is his throne, and the crucifixion is his enthronement.[21] In the synoptics, the revelation of Jesus' glory takes place not on Good Friday but on Easter Day.

While it is modern scholarship that has labeled Matthew, Mark, and Luke as the "synoptic gospels," the distance that separates them from John is not a modern discovery. Its recognition is as old as the four-gospel collection itself; the very fact of John's inclusion shows

15. John 11:1–57.
16. John 11:47–53.
17. John 14–16.
18. Mark 13; Matt. 24; Luke 21.
19. John 17:5.
20. John 12:34; 13:31–32.
21. John 19:19–22.

that the distance was felt to be a positive rather than a negative factor. The question is how and why that distance enhances the canonical collection rather than undermining it and making it incoherent.

The differences illustrated here may not all be of the same kind. It is unlikely that Jesus performed similar demonstrations in the temple at both the beginning and the end of his ministry. It is not unlikely that Jesus visited Jerusalem more than once in the course of his ministry. All the same, these differences show why it has proved so difficult—indeed, impossible—to construct out of the four gospels a credible account of Jesus' ministry in its actual historical sequence. Attempts to do just that long predate the modern concern to recover a "historical Jesus," and the motivation was similar. The gospels were deemed unsatisfactory in their present plural state, providing no coherent account of the historical life of Jesus but only the raw material for such an account. And so "gospel harmonies" were constructed in which the contents of all four gospels were blended together, in the hope that the differences and difficulties that seem to hinder access to the authentic life of Jesus would finally disappear. Yet gospel harmonies created far more problems than they solved. It seems that the fourfold gospel is not *intended* to provide a singular "life of Jesus" in which each incident and saying is assigned to its original historical context. Its relation to reality is more complex—and more interesting—than that.

In the course of his great commentary on the Gospel of John, Origen of Alexandria reflects on just these issues. One point of departure is the seemingly innocuous statement of John 2:12 that "after this [i.e., turning water into wine] Jesus went down to Capernaum with his mother, his brothers, and his disciples." Origen imagines himself in debate with those who take a high view of the gospels' historical reliability. He puts to them this question: When did Jesus first visit Capernaum?

If we ask when Jesus was first in Capernaum, our respondents, if they follow the words of Matthew and the other two, will say, "After the temptation, when he left Nazareth and came and dwelt in Capernaum by the sea." But how can they show that both accounts are true, the one given by Matthew and Mark, according to which it was because Jesus heard of John the Baptist's arrest that he departed to Galilee, and the one given by John, according to which the Baptist had not yet been thrown into prison but was baptizing in Aenon near Salim even some considerable time after Jesus' residence in Capernaum, when he had visited Jerusalem and departed for the Judean countryside?[22]

In Matthew, Jesus hears of John's arrest immediately after the forty days of temptation and departs for Galilee.[23] There he "leaves Nazareth" (although nothing is said of his arrival there) and chooses to reside instead in "Capernaum by the sea."[24] In John too, Jesus arrives in Capernaum and stays there for some time; he then travels to Jerusalem for the Passover.[25] Then he exercises a ministry of baptism in Judea that runs in parallel to John's,[26] for, as the evangelist notes, "John had not yet been thrown into prison."[27] Did Jesus' residence in Capernaum follow the arrest of John or precede it? Matthew takes one view, John the other. The Johannine statement that "John had not yet been thrown into prison" must respond to the assumption that John had already been arrested and imprisoned at the start of Jesus' ministry—an assumption based on the Matthean and Markan accounts. The later evangelist explicitly rejects the view that Jesus' ministry could only begin when John's had ended, claiming that the two ministries coexisted for a while in parallel and indeed in competition with each other.[28] This evangelist is aware of the synoptic version of events and considers it to be at best incomplete. Origen's point is not to side with one evangelist against the others but to illustrate a broader issue posed by the gospel collection. If our concern is with "historical reliability," we cannot be confident

22. Origen, *Commentary on John* 10.13.
23. Matt. 4:12.
24. Matt. 4:13.
25. John 2:12–13.
26. John 3:22–23.
27. John 3:24.
28. John 3:26.

that *any* of the various accounts actually delivers it. The problem is widespread:

> There are many other points at which the careful reader of the gospels will find that their narratives do not agree. . . . Disturbed by this discovery, the reader will either abandon the attempt to find all the gospels to be true, and—not wanting to conclude that *all* our information about our Lord is unreliable—will choose at random one of them to be his guide; or he will accept the four, and will consider that their truth is not to be sought in the outward and material letter.[29]

While similar issues arise among the synoptic accounts themselves, it is appropriate that Origen develops this argument in the context of a commentary on the Gospel of John. It is this gospel that most forcefully poses questions about the level on which the coherence of the four-gospel collection is to be found.[30]

The Johannine Eagle

Differences between the gospels can only be a positive rather than a negative factor, even and especially in the case of the difference that separates the first three gospels from the fourth. The fourfold gospel has been constructed in such a way as to embrace plural perspectives on the figure of Jesus and to rule out the assumption that a single perspective would testify to him more adequately. The plurality is not unlimited, however; the fixed figure four serves to exclude as well as include. Nor is the plurality unstructured; it is its three-plus-one structure that is our present concern. The evangelist symbol tradition provides a way to make sense of that structure.

The prophet Ezekiel sees a vision of a chariot-throne attended by four living creatures, each with four faces.[31] In the book of Revelation,

---

29. Origen, *Commentary on John* 10.14.
30. Origen's significance for a canonical reading of the gospels is rightly noted by B. Childs, *New Testament as Canon*, 146.
31. Ezek. 1:10.

Ezekiel's four identical four-faced creatures undergo a transformation.[32] John the seer is drawn up into heaven through an open door and sees a throne on which there sits one whose appearance so defies description that it can only be compared to precious stones. From the throne lightning and thunder issue forth, and in front of it there are seven burning torches and a glass-like sea. Around the central throne sit twenty-four gold-crowned, white-clad elders on thrones of their own. The space around the throne is shared with "four living creatures, full of eyes in front and behind."[33] The rims of Ezekiel's chariot wheels are also said to be "full of eyes all around,"[34] and this feature has now been transferred to the four living creatures themselves; the wheels have disappeared, for this throne is not intended to be mobile. More important, each of the four faces of Ezekiel's identical creatures has become a creature in its own right, so that they are now utterly different from one another. Rather than attending a chariot, they now lead the heavenly liturgy:

> The first living creature is like a lion, the second living creature is like a calf, the third living creature has a face like a human face, the fourth living creature is like a flying eagle. . . . Day and night without ceasing they sing, "Holy, holy, holy is the Lord God Almighty, who was and is and is to come."[35]

The evangelist symbol tradition can appeal to Ezekiel or to Revelation or to both. The Ezekiel passage has the advantage of an assured prophetic status; the Revelation passage provides a particularly impressive image of harmony and unity within extreme difference. Since Ezekiel's four faces are the same as the four creatures of Revelation, there is no need to choose. The order is slightly different, however: human, lion, calf, eagle in Ezekiel; lion, calf, human, eagle in Revelation.

32. Rev. 4:1–8.
33. Rev. 4:6.
34. Ezek. 1:18.
35. Rev. 4:7–8.

At this point we return briefly to Jerome. A few years after re-
cording the anecdote about the aged apostle John in his Galatians
commentary, Jerome produced his own edition of an old Latin commentary on the book of Revelation. Its author was Victorinus of
Pettau, who had died in the Diocletianic persecution in about 303,
nearly one hundred years before Jerome took up his work. In commenting on Revelation 4, Victorinus had followed Irenaeus's version
of the evangelist symbol tradition. In that original version of the
scheme, the human figure and the calf are assigned to Matthew and
Luke, and the lion and the eagle to John and Mark. Jerome accepts
the first two pairings but reverses the third and fourth. In place of
a Johannine lion and a Markan eagle, he substitutes a Markan lion
and a Johannine eagle. According to Victorinus,

> Mark opens thus: "The beginning of the gospel of Jesus Christ, as it
> is written in Isaiah." He starts from the flying Spirit, and so has the
> image of the flying eagle.
>
> The living creature like a lion is the Gospel according to John,
> because, after all the evangelists had preached Christ as made human,
> he preached him as God before he came down and took flesh, saying:
> "The Word was God." And because he cried out like a roaring lion,
> his proclamation bears the lion's face.[36]

These pairings are not very satisfactory. The flying eagle is not a
good image of the prophetic Spirit who spoke through Isaiah. And
it is hard to hear a lion's roar in "the Word was God." So Jerome
rewrites these passages as follows:

> Mark the Evangelist—opening thus: "The beginning of the gospel of
> Jesus Christ, as it is written in Isaiah the prophet, 'The voice of one
> crying in the wilderness'"—has the image of the lion.
>
> John the Evangelist, taking wing like an eagle, discourses of the
> Word of God.[37]

36. Victorinus, *Commentary on Revelation* (on Rev. 4:4).
37. Jerome/Victorinus, *Commentary on Revelation* (on Rev. 4:4).

In his original comment on John, Victorinus suggested that the fourth gospel was intended to complement and balance the first three by focusing on Christ's divinity rather than his humanity. Victorinus did not invent this idea himself but passed on a tradition that was already well known. According to this tradition, the fourfold gospel may be said to include either four perspectives on the figure of Jesus, symbolized by the four different creatures, or just two perspectives: one represented by the three texts that highlight Christ's human nature, the other by the single text that highlights his divine nature. Victorinus does not develop the point, and Jerome ignores it here. Yet Jerome's Johannine eagle enables his younger contemporary Augustine to develop this two-sided understanding of the canonical gospel in theologically fruitful and imaginative ways.

Augustine points to a basic difference between the flying eagle and its three colleagues:

> These three creatures—the lion, the human, and the calf—are all earthbound. It follows that the three corresponding evangelists are primarily concerned with what Christ did in the flesh and with his instructions for the conduct of this mortal life, addressed to those who still bear the burden of the flesh. John, on the other hand, flies like an eagle above the clouds of human weakness and gazes on the light of unchangeable truth with the sharpest and steadiest eyes, those of the heart.[38]

Augustine is not content here with a general contrast between Christ's human and divine natures. His concern is with *actions*: what Jesus did, but also what he instructs us to do by his teaching and example. It is Mark's gospel that is most consistently oriented to "what Christ did in the flesh," whereas Matthew's devotes the most attention to "instructions for the conduct of this mortal life." Yet Augustine is interested here not in comparisons between the earthbound gospels but in the contrast with the Johannine eagle. He can hardly mean that John is unconcerned with what Christ did in the flesh. Rather,

---

38. Augustine, *Harmony of the Evangelists* 1.6.9.

his point is that the Fourth Evangelist is enabled to see above and beyond the earthly life of Jesus to its context in the eternal Word's life with God, and the Father's will to draw all people to participate in that life. That is the "light of unchangeable truth" revealed to this evangelist.

The twofold structure of the gospel reflects both the two natures of Christ and the two faculties of the human mind. First, a fuller statement of the christological point:

> The first three evangelists present their diverse accounts of what Christ did in human flesh during his historical life, whereas John had in view above all the Lord's divinity, in which he is equal to the Father, and strove to emphasize this in his gospel so far as he thought it necessary for his readers. He is therefore borne up high above the other three, so that you may consider these as remaining on this earth below in order to engage with the human Christ, but John as ascending above the clouds covering the whole earth and attaining that pure heaven where, with sharpest and steadiest intellectual vision, he sees the Word of God who was in the beginning with God, through whom all things were made, and knows him as the one made flesh to dwell among us.[39]

The twofold structure of the gospel also reflects the structure of the human mind. There are, says Augustine,

> two faculties assigned to the human mind, one active, the other contemplative; one by which one journeys, the other by which one arrives; one by which one labors for purity of heart in hope of seeing God, the other by which one is at rest and sees God; one concerned with directions for the conduct of this temporal life, the other with instruction in that life which is eternal.[40]

A complex analogy takes shape between the dual, three-plus-one structure of the canonical gospel, the human and divine natures of Christ, and the active and contemplative faculties of the human mind.

39. Augustine, *Harmony of the Evangelists* 1.4.7.
40. Augustine, *Harmony of the Evangelists* 1.5.8.

Augustine turns here to his favorite image of life as a journey or pilgrimage from a foreign country to the true home, which is in God. In its two-sided testimony to Christ, the gospel orients us both to the journey's end and to right conduct along the way. The fourth gospel speaks of the journey's end—the goal and orientation of human existence—as "eternal life." Jesus, the Son, "has life in himself"[41] and comes into the world as "the bread of life" to give life to others.[42] It is as if the end comes to meet us on the way. Indeed, the end *becomes* the way: "I am the way, and the truth, and the life."[43] Eternal life is the goal of human existence not because an unending life after death is good or desirable in itself but "so that they may know you, the only true God, and Jesus Christ whom you have sent."[44]

In these words it is truly Jesus who speaks, but Jesus *according to John*. And so the evangelist himself can be associated with the flying eagle as, "with the sharpest and steadiest eyes," he "gazes on the light of unchangeable truth."

In the Beginning

Every narrative must start somewhere. Its narrator must select and isolate some point in time and space at which to begin. Whether that time and space is imaginary, as in fiction, or real, as in history writing, a starting point must be found within the totality of actual or conceivable occurrence—a moment in which leading features of the narrative to come can be highlighted and introduced to the reader. The beginning is the foundation on which a narrative is built.

All narratives must begin somewhere, and all four gospels reflect on their own beginnings. In three of them, the word "beginning" (*archē*) occurs at or near their beginnings. In Mark, it is the very first word: "Beginning of the gospel of Jesus Christ, Son of God."[45] In

41. John 5:26.
42. John 6:35.
43. John 14:6.
44. John 17:3.
45. Mark 1:1.

John, it is the second word: *En archē*, "In the beginning." Here the beginning of the gospel echoes the beginning of the book of Genesis. In the single long sentence that forms Luke's preface, a reference to "the beginning" occurs about halfway through. This evangelist identifies three stages in the history that leads up to his own composition, mentioning them in reverse order. The third stage is that of the written gospel, in which Luke adds his own work to the efforts of his predecessors. The second stage is the oral transmission of the Jesus tradition in the apostolic preaching. The first stage consists of the events communicated in that preaching. This sequence of events is communicated by eyewitnesses who participated in them "from the beginning."[46]

Only in Matthew's beginning is the word "beginning" absent. There it is replaced with a near synonym, *genesis*, "becoming." Genesis is the name of a book, but Matthew's opening words, *biblos geneseōs*, refer not to the book of Genesis but to the "book of the genealogy of Jesus Christ."[47] The opening Greek phrase is derived from Genesis, however. At the start of Genesis 5, "the book of the genealogy of Adam" is announced.[48] The book of Adam's genealogy is concerned with his descendants, the book of Jesus' genealogy is concerned with his ancestors, and the combination of the two shows Jesus' full integration into the human race—specifically that branch of it that traces its descent from Abraham, Isaac, and Jacob.

Like Matthew, John opens his gospel with a two-word phrase borrowed from Genesis. In the original contexts, the phrase used by Matthew speaks of the origins of the human race, the one used by John of the origin of all things: "In the beginning, God created the heavens and the earth."[49] In John, however, the reference is not to the event of creation but to that which already "was" when that primal event took place: "In the beginning *was* the Word." That "was" is twice repeated in the rest of this three-part sentence: "and the Word

46. Luke 1:2.
47. Matt. 1:1.
48. Gen. 5:1a.
49. Gen. 1:1.

was with God, and the Word *was* God."[50] In the next verse, the first and second parts of the opening sentence are bound even more closely together: "This one was in the beginning with God."[51] That which was in the beginning is eternal. There was no time when it was not. Being eternal, it is also divine: eternity is an exclusive attribute of divinity, so an entity that is eternally with God must itself be God. According to the Fourth Evangelist, that is the case with the Word which "became flesh" in the person of Jesus Christ.[52] Of the two gospels attributed to apostles, John's begins from the eternal Word, Matthew's from the human, Jewish Jesus. The eternal Word is Jesus; the human Jesus is the eternal divine Word. Such statements are an offense to other views of deity, past or present, monotheistic or polytheistic. For communities that acknowledge the fourfold gospel, they are nonnegotiable truth.

John's beginning may also be compared with Mark's. In both cases, statements about the "beginning" are followed by a reference to John the Baptist. According to the Fourth Evangelist, "There came a man sent from God whose name was John."[53] In Mark this figure is identified as "John the Baptizer."[54] Matthew alters this to the familiar "John the Baptist" and is followed in this by Luke.[55] In the fourth gospel, John the Baptist is simply "John." Here his activity as a baptizer is marginal, and the focus instead is on his *witness* or *testimony*: "He came for testimony, so as to bear witness to the light, so that all might believe through him."[56] In this gospel the purpose of John's baptism is the disclosure that the previously unrecognized Jesus is the Son of God. That disclosure is made first to John himself, as he beholds the descent of the dove-like Spirit, and then through John to those who hear his testimony: "Behold, the Lamb of God

50. John 1:1.
51. John 1:2.
52. John 1:14, 17.
53. John 1:6.
54. Mark 1:4.
55. Matt. 3:1; Luke 7:20, 33.
56. John 1:7.

who takes away the sin of the world."[57] As presented by Mark, John
the Baptist's testimony to Jesus is indirect. John prepares the way of
the Lord as he speaks of the coming one who is greater than he and
as Jesus submits to his baptism.[58] The Fourth Evangelist makes this
indirect testimony direct and explicit. Rather than following Matthew
and Luke by adding birth stories, he offers his own interpretation of
Mark's decision to begin from the figure of John the Baptist. John
becomes an apostolic figure, sent from God to bear witness; his testimony to Jesus' identity anticipates the later apostolic testimony.[59]
The communication of the gospel by those who have seen and heard
the original divine disclosure is integrated into the gospel story itself.

Comparison between John's beginning and Luke's brings to light
two contrasting settings for Jesus' ministry. Luke is concerned to set
the gospel events in a broad historical and geographical context. John
the Baptist is born in the days of Herod king of Judea.[60] Jesus is born
in Bethlehem because of a decision taken in Rome by the emperor
Augustus.[61] The ministry of John the Baptist is dated from the fifteenth
year of Augustus's successor, Tiberius, at which point King Herod has
also been succeeded by the tetrarchs Herod (Antipas) in Galilee and
Philip in the regions of Iturea and Trachonitis.[62] These historical and
geographical coordinates assure the reader that Jesus belongs within
the real world and that he is not a semilegendary figure who lived
long ago in some far-distant place. In John too, the Word *became
flesh*—that is, an individual human being limited and defined by a
specific context. Here, however, it is *the Word* that became flesh. The
Word, who was with God in the beginning, is equally present to all
contexts, since "all things were made through him and without him
was nothing made."[63] His presence in a particular time and place is

57. John 1:29; cf. vv. 26–34.
58. Mark 1:2–9.
59. John 17:20; 20:21.
60. Luke 1:5.
61. Luke 2:1.
62. Luke 3:1.
63. John 1:3.

also his presence in and for the world: "He was in the world, and the world was made through him."[64] Even John the Baptist now has a role that extends to the whole world. He was sent from God "so that *all* might believe through him,"[65] that is, so that the world may believe that Jesus is from God through the testimony of his witnesses. The object of this testimony is the specific individual Jesus, who is also the light that "comes into the world" and "shines in the darkness."[66] Within the fourfold gospel, there is no contradiction between the limited context established by Luke's names, dates, and places and John's universal horizons.

64. John 1:10.
65. John 1:7.
66. John 1:5, 9.

Part 2

⊕

Convergences

Over much of the route between beginnings and endings, the first three evangelists keep company with one another. Along the way there are significant differences of order and wording; a great deal of material is common to Matthew and Luke but not to Mark; and some further material is unique to Matthew, Luke, or (occasionally) Mark. In spite of variations, however, a common sequence may easily be identified.

John remains aloof. From the beginning he goes his own way, with only occasional points of contact with his colleagues. It is only toward the end—from the triumphal entry onward—that all four gospels begin to converge, and that convergence becomes systematic only at the moment of Jesus' betrayal and arrest. The route from Gethsemane to the empty tomb is traversed by all four evangelists together, an indication of the supreme importance of the events in which Jesus fulfills his vocation as Savior of the world.

If the fourfold testimony to these events is to have its full effect, a detailed analysis of gospel interrelations is required. Such an analysis would make it easy and natural for a reader to turn to parallel passages in the various gospels so that an individual evangelist's perspective can be enriched by the others. That would be especially desirable in the case of the passion events, in which the relationship between the texts is unusually intricate. Just such an analysis of gospel interrelations was carried out by Eusebius of Caesarea in the fourth century. It marked a major step forward in the ongoing attempt to show the four-gospel collection to be credible, demonstrating the harmonious order underlying the surface confusion.

That credibility is not apparent to all, however. In the early Christian centuries as in the present, it may be claimed that the gospels falsify the world itself with their untenable claims about imagined supernatural agencies and actions. The final question for readers of the gospels is whether—and under what conditions—a convergence can be identified between the texts and the reality about which they claim to disclose the truth.

5

Four Gospels, One Book

All four canonical gospels conclude with a full account of Jesus' suffering and death and more fragmentary narratives relating to his resurrection. While there is general agreement about the goal of the gospel story, the evangelists differ over the question of where it should begin. From the perspective of an individual evangelist, those differences may have been ideologically significant. Matthew presumably intended not to complement Mark but to correct his view that Jesus' messiahship can be traced no further back than the descent of the Spirit following his baptism. It is only within a fourfold gospel that Matthew, Mark, Luke, and John can and must be seen as complementary, their differences enhancing and enriching the truth of the message rather than undermining it. The fourfold gospel is greater than the sum of its parts.

Early readers found in the four different beginnings a key to each gospel's individuality. From these beginnings they learned that Jesus must be viewed from the plural perspectives represented by the four living creatures around the divine throne: one with a human face (representing the first gospel, which opens by retracing the roots of

Jesus' Jewish humanity), one with the face of a lion (the second gospel, with its threatening roar from the desert), one with the face of a calf (the third gospel, which starts, as it finishes, in the place of sacrifice), and one with the face of an eagle (the fourth gospel, which soars into the heavens to behold the eternal divine Word). These four transcendent angelic powers—identified by the seer John both with the cherubim of Ezekiel and the seraphim of Isaiah—are all wholly absorbed in the praise of the same object, but they view it differently. The same is true of the earthly books of which they are the heavenly patrons and symbols: they present not four Christs but one Christ seen through four different pairs of eyes.

The four heavenly beings reflect the different gospel openings, but they also symbolize gospel differences as a whole—everything that makes each gospel itself rather than one of the others. In the canonical gospel the same story is told and retold in four different ways, and sameness and difference are interwoven throughout, even in the smallest units of text. Almost everywhere a contrast may be found between one gospel and another, illuminating both texts and highlighting the interpretative work that has made each what it uniquely is. Yet where there is a contrast, there will also be a parallel or analogy. If there were no contrasts or differences, the result would be not four gospels but four identical copies of the same gospel. If there were no parallels or analogies, there would be no singular "gospel according to . . ."

The question is how this complex interweaving of difference and sameness is to be made comprehensible and fruitful for reading the texts. The symbolism generated by gospel openings provides an indispensable image of gospel diversity and unity, marking out the space within which interpretation is to be practiced, but another approach is needed if the play of perspectives is to be analyzed in detail. What is required is, simply, a *cross-referencing system* enabling a reader to navigate quickly and easily from a gospel passage to its parallel or parallels elsewhere. Without some such system, the different gospel sequences make it difficult even for an experienced reader to find whatever parallel passages there may be. It is important to be able to do so: these passages are not just loosely related to each other; they are different versions of the same material. If one takes the fourfold gospel seriously, one will want to know whether, say, Matthew's story of Jesus' walking on the water has a parallel in any other gospel and, if so, what new angles the different versions might bring to light. A cross-referencing system will guide the reader from Matthew 14:22–33 to Mark 6:45–52 and John 6:16–21. It will also spare one the frustration of searching in vain for this story in Luke. More than any other part of the Old or New Testaments, the four gospels *demand* to be fitted out with cross-references.

At some point in the early decades of the fourth century, that demand was met. An ingenious system of cross-references was devised by Eusebius of Caesarea, who is as important a figure in the development of the four-gospel collection as he is for the history of the early church. His system is superior to the kind found in most modern Bibles, as it locates the cross-references within a comprehensive analysis of ten different combinations in which the gospels are related to one another. Underappreciated now, Eusebius's significance for the study of the gospels was recognized in ancient gospel books that not only incorporate his so-called canon tables but also on occasion dignify him with a portrait, even placing him on a level similar to that of the evangelists themselves. He is the key figure in the development of the four-gospel codex, the book that not only contains all four gospels but—in Eusebius's edition—also provides a rationale for their inclusion between the covers of a single volume.[1]

To retrieve Eusebius's now largely neglected achievement, we begin with a portrait that survives in a sixth- or seventh-century Latin gospel codex—though this is a portrait not of Eusebius but of Luke.

---

1. For an illuminating discussion of Eusebius's significance for the development of the codex, see A. Grafton and M. Williams, *Christianity and the Transformation of the Book*, 133–243; and, for the wider context, M. Wallraff, *Kodex und Kanon*.

The Evangelist: Portrait and Artist

In or around the year 601 CE, Bishop Augustine of Canterbury received welcome confirmation that, in faraway Rome, Pope Gregory I continued to support his mission to the pagan English. Impressed by Augustine's achievements over the four years since his arrival in the southeast of Britain, Gregory sent additional personnel to assist him in his labors, together with—as Bede informs us—"all things in general that were necessary for the worship and service of the church." These included sacred vessels, vestments, and relics, "besides many books."[2] The books necessary for the worship and service of the church would surely have included the most important books of Holy Scripture, including the gospels.

One such gospel book survives and is known as the "St. Augustine Gospels." The tradition that it originated in sixth-century Italy and is one of the books sent by Gregory is plausible, although impossible to prove. For around nine hundred years the book was treasured in the monastery Augustine founded in Canterbury. After the monastery was dissolved in 1538, the book found its way into the collection of Archbishop Matthew Parker, who bequeathed it to Corpus Christi College, Cambridge, in whose Parker Library it remains to this day. The book is missing much of its introductory material and artwork, but its Latin gospel text is intact, along with standard supplements such as gospel prefaces and *capitula* lists (i.e., tables of contents).[3] Just two of the original illuminated pages still survive.[4] The first of these is located at folio 125, after the end of Mark and immediately before the preface to Luke. This page consists of a sequence of twelve scenes relating to the passion, from Jesus' raising of Lazarus and his triumphal entry into Jerusalem to the bearing of the cross to Golgotha. The second page is found shortly afterward, at folio 129,

2. Bede, *Ecclesiastical History of the English Nation* 1.29.
3. Full details in P. McGurk, *Latin Gospel Books*, 25–26.
4. The images are easily available online (search for "St. Augustine Gospels"). High-quality images of the entire volume may be viewed at https://parkerweb.stanford .edu/parker/actions/page_turner.do?ms_no=286. See also F. Wormald, *Miniatures in the Gospel of St Augustine*.

following the preface and *capitula* to Luke and directly opposite the
beginning of the gospel text. It consists of a portrait of the evangelist
seated within a four-pillared structure surmounted by an arch that
houses a winged calf—the symbol that identifies Luke as Luke. The
evangelist displays an open book to the viewer but does not make
direct eye contact, gazing pensively somewhere to the viewer's left,
his right hand supporting his chin.

Between each pair of pillars on either side of the evangelist are
three rectangular panels, each of which is divided horizontally by a
wavy line. These panels depict a total of twelve gospel-related scenes,
and they are accompanied by captions to identify them. Each panel
measures about 3 x 2 centimeters, and each of the paired images is
therefore on average only 1.5 centimeters high. In the first scene, an
angel appears to a bearded elderly man standing behind a small altar.
The caption reads: *Zacharias turbatus est* ("Zechariah was troubled").
The scene depicted corresponds to Luke 1:11–12:

> And there appeared to him an angel of the Lord standing to the right
> of the altar of incense. And Zechariah was troubled when he saw him,
> and fear fell upon him.

The sacrificial setting at the start of Luke's narrative links the seated
evangelist to the calf symbol in the arch above. Yet this sequence of images is not only concerned with the gospel opening. In the lower scene
on the first panel, Mary addresses the child Jesus—seated between two
adult male figures, one of whom might be Joseph—with the words *Fili,
quid fecisti nobis sic* ("Son, why have you done this to us?"). The first
panel thus brings together scenes from the beginning and end of Luke's
infancy narrative,[5] which concludes where it begins, in the temple.

Another paired beginning and ending occurs in the second panel,
located directly beneath the first. In the upper half, Jesus addresses
the crowds while seated in a boat (*hic sedens in navi docebat eos*).[6]

5. Luke 1:11–12; 2:48.
6. Cf. Luke 5:3.

In the lower half, Peter falls at Jesus' feet and begs him to depart
(*Petrus procidit ad genua Iesu*).[7] The reference is to the uniquely
Lukan version of the call of Peter, in which Jesus' preaching from
the boat is followed by a miraculous catch of fish, Peter's terrified
response ("Depart from me, for I am a sinful man, O Lord"), and
Jesus' call ("Do not be afraid, from now on you will be catching
people").[8]

Two of the remaining eight images are easily identifiable, even
without consulting the captions. In the top half of the third panel,
the body of a young man is being carried out of a city gate on a bier.
He is the son of the widow of Nain, and the artist has captured the
moment when Jesus halts the bier with a touch and says, "Young
man, I say to you, arise!"[9] At the end of the sequence of panels, in
the bottom half of the sixth panel and to the right of the seated
evangelist, Jesus addresses a man standing in a tree who can only be
Zacchaeus: "Zacchaeus, make haste and come down, for I must stay
at your house today."[10]

The accounts of Zechariah's vision, the child Jesus in the temple,
Peter's plea to be left alone, the resuscitation at Nain, and the meeting
with Zacchaeus have one thing in common: they are all unique to
Luke. As we shall see, the same is true of the rest of the series. The
seated evangelist presides over an exhibition of images inspired by
his own work. In his gospel as a whole, the material he shares with
one or more of the other evangelists is much more extensive than
material unique to his work; but not one of the twelve images depicts
an event narrated by another evangelist. There is here no baptism in
the river Jordan, feeding of the five thousand, or transfiguration—all
events that early Christian artists liked to portray. Neither is there any
particular emphasis on the beginning of the gospel, in spite of the
image of Zechariah's vision with which the series opens. Placed on
the page opposite the beginning of Luke's text, the evangelist portrait

7. Cf. Luke 5:8.
8. Luke 5:10.
9. Luke 7:14.
10. Luke 19:5.

and the accompanying image sequence anticipate episodes scattered throughout the text, from chapter 1 (Zechariah) to chapter 19 (Zacchaeus). This is a different way of identifying the distinctively Lukan contribution to gospel writing, one based on careful analysis of the text rather than the traditional evangelist symbols.

Prefatory to a Gospel

The artist did not have to carry out this textual analysis for himself. Rather, he made use of the "canons" or "canon tables" of Eusebius—lists of enumerated gospel sections, beginning with those that are common to all four gospels (canon I) and ending with sections unique to each individual gospel (canon X).[11] In canons II–IV, Eusebius lists sections common to three gospels (II: Matthew–Mark–Luke; III: Matthew–Luke–John; IV: Matthew–Mark–John). Canons I and II contain 74 and 111 sets of parallel sections, respectively, and are much more densely populated than canons III and IV, with just 22 and 25 sets of parallels. Canons V–IX list sections common to two gospels, in the combinations Matthew–Luke (V: 82 sections), Matthew–Mark (VI: 47 sections), Matthew–John (VII: 7 sections), Luke–Mark (VIII: 13 sections), and Luke–John (IX: 21 sections). In canon X, unparalleled material is listed for each gospel (Matthew, 62 sections; Mark, 19; Luke, 72; John, 96). Eusebius finds no material worth listing for the combinations Mark–Luke–John or Mark–John. By grouping the unique passages into a single subdivided "canon" or list, Eusebius is able to keep the number of the canons to ten, a number that has symbolic significance as the sum of the four main categories of gospel interrelations: passages shared by four gospels, by three gospels, by two gospels, and those unique to a single gospel—that is, 4 + 3 + 2 + 1 = 10.

11. The canon tables are printed along with Eusebius's prefatory "Letter to Carpianus" in NA[28], 89–94*, and in earlier editions from the seventh onward. The text is based on canon tables in early Greek, Latin, and Gothic manuscripts and does not derive from the print editions whose variants it cites. See E. Nestle, "Die Eusebianische Evangelien-Synopse."

The twelve uniquely Lukan passages depicted in the St. Augustine Gospels have been selected from the seventy-two sections in Eusebius's canon X_3 and are listed in table 5.1. Without Eusebius's systematic analysis, many of these passages would be difficult to identify as uniquely Lukan. Then as now, most readers or hearers of the gospels would be familiar with the story of the resuscitation of the young man at Nain but would probably not be able to identify it confidently as distinctive to Luke. Given this dependence on Eusebius, it is also possible to identify passages that the artist chose *not* to depict. Zechariah's vision is included (Eus. X_3, *1*),[12] as is Mary's rebuke to the child Jesus in the temple (Eus. X_3, *5*), but a whole series of intervening events is passed over (Eus. X_3, *3* = Luke 1:36–2:46), as is the distinctive Lukan account of Jesus' preaching in the synagogue in Nazareth (Luke 4:16–30 = Eus. X_3, *18, 20, 22*). Jesus' teaching from a boat and Peter's terrified response to the miraculous catch belong to the same Lukan story (Luke 5:1–11) but are depicted separately in the image series because Eusebius has assigned them different section numbers (Eus. X_3, *29, 31*); the intervening account of the miraculous catch is assigned to canon IX on account of its Johannine parallel (Luke 5:4–7 = John 21:1–6). In all but the first of the twelve images, an encounter between Jesus and one or more individuals is depicted. Eusebius's canon X does not determine the selection of episodes depicted, but it does make the selection possible. In doing so, it also makes possible a new approach to the distinctiveness of the individual gospel, one that attempts to do justice to the text as a whole rather than focusing exclusively on its opening.

In this ancient gospel codex the evangelist portrait is the third and final element in the introductory material preceding the Latin text of Luke's gospel. Turning the pages back from the evangelist portrait, we find five pages devoted to an enumerated summary of the entire contents of the gospel (not just passages unique to Luke). The Eusebian numbering tracks the relationship with other gospels, but this second system is based on this gospel's internal

---

12. Italicized numbers indicate the Eusebian enumeration of gospel passages.

Table 5.1. Luke Sequence
(St. Augustine Gospels, Luke portrait, folio 129v)

Left Side	Right Side
1.1 Zechariah and the angel (Luke 1:11–12; Eus. X$_3$, 1)*	4.1 "And who is my neighbor?" (Luke 10:29–37; Eus. X$_3$, 122)
1.2 Mary rebukes the child Jesus in the temple (Luke 2:48–49; Eus. X$_3$, 5)	4.2 "Blessed is the womb that bore you . . ." (Luke 11:27–28; Eus. X$_3$, 131)
2.1 Teaching from the boat (Luke 5:3; Eus. X$_3$, 29)	5.1 "Teacher, tell my brother to divide the inheritance with me." (Luke 12:13–21; Eus. X$_3$, 149)
2.2 Peter falls at Jesus' knees (Luke 5:8; Eus. X$_3$, 31)	5.2 The parable of the fig tree; the woman bent double (Luke 13:6–13; Eus. X$_3$, 164)
3.1 Raising the widow of Nain's son (Luke 7:12–15; Eus. X$_3$, 67)	6.1 Healing of the man with dropsy (Luke 14:2–4; Eus. X$_3$, 176)
3.2 "No one who puts his hand to the plow . . ." (Luke 9:61–62; Eus. X$_3$, 106)	6.2 Jesus and Zacchaeus (Luke 19:1–9; Eus. X$_3$, 225)

*Eus. X$_3$, 1 = Eusebius's canon table X, passages unique to each gospel (here Luke's, hence X$_3$), followed by section number.

organization—like the more recent system of chapters and verses, of which it is a forerunner. Continuing to turn back, we find two pages devoted to a prologue that introduces the evangelist and explains what led him to write:

Luke, by birth a Syrian from Antioch and by profession a doctor, was a disciple of the apostles who afterward followed Paul until his martyrdom, serving God blamelessly. For he never had a wife or children and died in Bithynia at the age of seventy-four, full of the Holy Spirit. When gospels had already been written, first by Matthew in Judea and then by Mark in Italy, he wrote this gospel at the prompting of the Holy Spirit in the regions of Achaia, indicating at the outset that other gospels had already been written. In addition to the orderly presentation of the gospel events, the main purpose of his work was to ensure that—the coming of God in the flesh being manifested in all perfection—the faithful among the Greeks should not be held back by an attraction merely to the law, following after Jewish fictions, or fall away from the truth by being seduced and enticed by the folly of heretical falsehood. Beginning his gospel from the nativity of John, he indicated to whom he was writing [i.e., Theophilus] and in whom as an elect one he was writing, testifying that he was bringing to completion what had been begun by others.[13]

That, at least, was how the anonymous fourth-century author of a popular set of gospel prologues imagined the origins of Luke's gospel. Once again the distinctiveness of this gospel comes to the fore. In relation to Matthew and Mark, it was composed by a different individual in a different place, at a different time and in different circumstances. The prologue, the summary of contents, and the evangelist portrait are typical of ancient four-gospel codices, and they give the lie to any assumption that the distinctiveness of one gospel vis-à-vis the others is an exclusively modern concern. The three introductory elements are closely integrated, with the prologue oriented toward the evangelist's biography, the summary toward the text itself, and the portrait with its accompanying images pointing both to the text and to its author.

Lucas Syrus natione Antiocensis arte medicus ("Luke, by birth a Syrian from Antioch and by profession a doctor"): in the St. Augustine Gospels, the first two lines of the prologue to Luke are written in red ink and enlarged letters. Here, at the opening of the Luke section of this four-gospel codex, the first word is given to the name of the evangelist. The left-hand (or verso) page is left blank. The format is the same at the opening of the Mark section: a blank page on the left, and on the right (recto) the opening of the Mark prologue with the words *Marcus evangelista dei et Petri in baptismate filius* ("Mark,

---

13. This gospel preface is from a set known as the "Monarchian Prologues," included in a large number of Latin gospel manuscripts. Latin text in K. Aland, ed., *Synopsis Quattuor Evangeliorum*, 538–39. The prefaces have been attributed to Priscillian of Avila but are listed as "spurious" in the latest edition of his writings (M. Conti, ed., *Priscillian of Avila*, ix; texts with translations, 251–57).

evangelist of God and Peter's son in baptism"). In the case of John, the scribe fails to complete the ending of Luke on the recto page, and the last few words therefore spill over onto a page intended to be left blank. Facing it is the prologue to John: *Hic est Iohannes evangelista unus ex discipulis dei* ("This is John the evangelist, one of the disciples of God" [i.e., of Jesus]). No doubt the missing pages of the Matthew introductory material opened in the same way, with a blank page on the left and the prologue on the right: *Mattheus ex Iudaeis, sicut in ordine primus ponitur, evangelium in Iudaea primus scripsit* ("Just as Matthew, who was of Jewish origin, is placed first in order, so he was the first to write a gospel, doing so in Judea").[14] In each case, the blank left-hand page signals the beginning not just of a chapter or section but of a complete book. The gospel codex contains four separate books, which more commonly circulated individually but are here bound together into a single volume. As the blank pages signify, the four books remain separate even when bound together. The prefatory material—which in Luke's case includes the evangelist portrait—highlights their separateness.

The question is whether a codex such as the St. Augustine Gospels can express the unity of the four-gospel collection at a deeper level than that of the binding. To answer this question, we need to take a closer look at Eusebius's canon tables.

Order out of Chaos

To someone reading consecutively through the Gospels of Matthew, Mark, Luke, and John for the first time, the relationship between them might well seem chaotic. As Matthew's narrative is succeeded by Mark's, the reader encounters what appears to be the same or similar events, differently narrated and in a different order. In Matthew, as an attentive reader may note, the divine voice at Jesus' baptism announces, "This is my beloved son." In Mark, the words

14. As Margaret Mitchell points out, patristic authorship traditions assign the gospels to different places and contexts ("Patristic Counter-Evidence").

are addressed to Jesus himself: "You are my beloved son."[15] In Greek and Latin as in English, this is a difference of just two short words: *houtos estin* or *hic est* ("this is") is replaced by *su ei* or *tu es* ("you are"). Yet the difference profoundly affects the sense. In Matthew, Jesus cleanses a leper after delivering his Sermon on the Mount and, on arrival in Capernaum, heals the centurion's servant and Peter's mother-in-law.[16] In Mark there is no trace of the Sermon or the centurion, and Peter's mother-in-law and the leper are healed in reverse order.[17] There is also a new story about an exorcism in the Capernaum synagogue that is absent from Matthew.[18] The complications continue to multiply as the reader proceeds through Mark and on into Luke and John. To the ordinary reader, whether ancient or modern, the narratives appear to weave in and out of one another without rhyme or reason.

For a reader who is not prepared simply to acquiesce in this seeming chaos, the resources of modern scholarship provide often-illuminating results. The key move is to reverse the traditional order of Matthew–Mark to Mark–Matthew and to understand the relationship of the two texts in genetic terms. Rather than merely noting differences, one *explains* them by interpreting them as an editor's deliberate changes to his source, rewording, rearranging, adding, or omitting, as seemed appropriate. Where Matthew and Luke are seen as editors of Mark, comprehensible and rational editorial strategies come to light. Yet this genetic method of reducing seeming chaos to relative order is only as good as the hypotheses on which it rests. While Markan priority seems immune to serious challenge, that is not the case with the second pillar of the modern scholarly edifice, the "Q" hypothesis, which alleges the independent use, by Matthew and Luke, of a second, lost source alongside Mark. Can we be sure that Luke was ignorant of Matthew? How is it that so much of the non-Markan content of Luke makes such excellent sense on the

15. Cf. Matt. 3:17; Mark 1:11.
16. Matt. 8:1–17.
17. Mark 1:29–31, 40–45.
18. Mark 1:21–28.

assumption of a somewhat critical and independent engagement with Matthew?[19]

The "synoptic problem" will rightly continue to be debated, and further clarifications may yet be achieved. In its concern with sources, however, it relates to the precanonical stage of gospel origins, prior to the collective decision to separate out four of the various attempts to write the gospel and to endow them with authorial identities and a shared authoritative status. As part of the fourfold gospel, the text that is now "Mark" is no longer a mere source for "Matthew" and "Luke" but an independent work in its own right that takes its place alongside the others. The assumed chronological order of Matthew–Mark–Luke–John does not imply any genetic relationship between them. The almost complete absence of genetic hypotheses in the ancient church represents not so much a mistake about the true nature of the gospels, needing to be corrected by modern scholarship, but rather a *decision* about how the canonical gospels are to be read—as independent yet parallel texts whose interrelations justify both their continued existence as separate entities and their incorporation into a single definitive embodiment of the gospel message.

That decision leaves open the question of how gospel interrelations are to be made comprehensible. It was the achievement of Eusebius of Caesarea to show, through his canon tables, how the apparent chaos of the four different tellings of the same story can be reduced to rational and harmonious order. The canon tables represent both a scholarly tool (a cross-referencing system that enables one to compare and contrast parallel passages) and an intellectual justification for the very concept of a fourfold gospel. Where this cross-referencing system has been installed, a four-gospel codex is no longer just a collection of four distinct books that happen to be bound together between the covers of a single volume. At every point, the gospel text is accompanied by a numerical system that relates a given passage to its equivalents in other gospels. Each evangelist is constantly shadowed by the others; the enumeration invites the reader to break off from

19. See F. Watson, *Gospel Writing*, 117–216.

the linear reading process and to turn back or forward to parallel passages that shed new light on the passage under consideration. In following the links, the reader becomes aware that the network of interrelations is not a chaotic tangle but an orderly structure with ten major categories that can be grasped without difficulty. The analysis that brings this network to light is based not on source-critical hypotheses but on the texts as they stand. Eusebius's analysis was found to be so illuminating that it was incorporated into gospel codices across the Christian world of late antiquity, from Ireland and Britain to Syria and Armenia, Egypt and Ethiopia.[20] Far from being relegated to an appendix, the canon tables are placed in a position of honor at or near the beginning of these four-gospel codices, often framed within elaborately decorated arches and arcades. Even before reaching the prefatory material to Matthew, the reader is encouraged to contemplate a set of artistic and numerical representations of the fourfold gospel in its underlying order and beauty.

Parallels and Numbers

Eusebius designed his cross-referencing system to be incorporated into a single-codex edition of the gospels, and it is this edition that underlies all the later vernacular texts in which canon tables are included.[21] These texts also preserve the preface addressed to an individual named Carpianus in which Eusebius succinctly explains his system and how to operate it. Here he acknowledges his debt to the scholarly work of a predecessor, Ammonius of Alexandria, who created a gospel synopsis in which parallel passages were placed alongside each other in four columns. In the first column Ammonius had placed the complete text of Matthew, and parallel passages in other

20. Greek, Latin, Syriac, and Gothic canon tables are discussed by C. Nordenfalk, *Die spätantiken Kanontafeln*. For Ethiopia, see my contribution to a forthcoming work on the Garima Gospels (ca. sixth century): J. McKenzie and F. Watson, *Early Illuminated Gospel Books*.

21. For the discussion that follows, see also M. Crawford, "Ammonius of Alexandria."

gospels were therefore forced to conform to the Matthean sequence, which does not necessarily correspond to their own. Non-Matthean material—that is, passages common to Luke and Mark (Eusebius's canon VIII), Luke and John (canon IX), and passages unique to Mark, Luke, and John (canon $X_{2,3,4}$)—was probably relegated to the end of Ammonius's work. It is this dismantling of the non-Matthean gospels that not only evoked Eusebius's criticism but also inspired his own work. In his own words:

> With impressive diligence and industry, Ammonius of Alexandria bequeathed to us a fourfold gospel in which he placed alongside the Gospel of Matthew the similar passages from the other evangelists. The inevitable result was that the orderly sequence of the other three was destroyed, making a consecutive reading impossible. In order that, with the entire content and sequence of the others left intact, you may know the passages in each evangelist where they were led in their love of truth to speak of the same things, we have taken our starting point from the labors of the individual previously mentioned while devising a different scheme, drawing up the ten canons attached below.[22]

Eusebius constructed his ten canons directly from Ammonius's synopsis. With the help of a simple example—the Beatitudes, which open Jesus' inaugural sermon in both Matthew and Luke—it is possible to reconstruct the route he took from his predecessor's synopsis to his own canon tables by retracing his parallel numbers back to the equivalent texts in their four-column format. This will lead to further insight into how gospel parallels work and will set the scene for the next two chapters of this book, in which Eusebius's system will help to clarify the fourfold gospel testimony to the events of Jesus' passion.

1. Ammonius's synopsis was probably formatted in four columns throughout, with space left blank where no parallels were to be found. As indicated by the angled brackets in table 5.2, he had to reverse the order of the second and third Lukan beatitudes so as to conform

---

22. NA^{28}, 89–90* (my translation).

them to Matthew. In the absence of parallel beatitudes in Mark or
John, their columns are left blank.

Table 5.2. Ammonius's Synopsis

Matthew 5:1–6	Mark	Luke 6:20, 21b, 21a	John
And seeing the crowds he went up into the mountain, and when he sat down his disciples came to him. And opening his mouth he taught them, saying: "Blessed are the poor in spirit, for theirs is the kingdom of heaven.		And lifting up his eyes to the disciples, he said: "Blessed are the poor, for yours is the kingdom of God.	
"Blessed are the meek, for they shall inherit the earth.			
"Blessed are those who mourn, for they shall be comforted.		<"Blessed are those who weep now, for you shall laugh.>	
"Blessed are those who hunger and thirst for righteousness, for they shall be satisfied."		"Blessed are those who hunger now, for you shall be satisfied."	

2. Studying the contents of Ammonius's columns, Eusebius notes
that the gospels relate to each other in ten different ways within four
broader categories. For some passages, there is parallel text in all
four columns; in others, in three columns (whether Matthew–Mark–
Luke, Matthew–Luke–John, or Matthew–Mark–John); in others, in
two (Matthew–Luke, Matthew–Mark, Matthew–John, and, toward
the end, Luke–Mark, Luke–John); and, in other cases, text appears
in a single column (Matthew throughout, Mark, Luke, John in the
post-Matthean appendix). Having enumerated these ten different relationships, Eusebius then works systematically through Ammonius's
synopsis, inserting the appropriate number wherever the relationship
between gospels changes (table 5.3). The sections are therefore determined entirely by a gospel's shifting relationship to other gospels, not
by its own natural divisions.[23] It is the presence in Luke of the blessing

23. This often misunderstood point is rightly emphasized by H. von Soden, *Die
Schriften des Neuen Testaments*, 390.

of the poor and the absence of the blessing of the meek that assigns one beatitude to canon V (Matthew–Luke) and the other to canon X_1 (Matthew alone) and so creates a section break in the Matthean text.

Table 5.3. Addition of Canon Numbers
(V: Matthew–Luke; X: one gospel only)

Matthew 5:1–6	Mark	Luke 6:20–21	John
X And seeing the crowds he went up into the mountain, and when he sat down his disciples came to him.			
V And opening his mouth he taught them, saying: "Blessed are the poor in spirit, for theirs is the kingdom of heaven.		V And lifting up his eyes to the disciples, he said: "Blessed are the poor, for yours is the kingdom of God.	
X "Blessed are the meek, for they shall inherit the earth.			
V "Blessed are those who mourn, for they shall be comforted.		<V "Blessed are those who weep now, for you shall laugh.>	
V "Blessed are those who hunger and thirst for righteousness, for they shall be satisfied."		V "Blessed are those who hunger now, for you shall be satisfied."	

3. After inserting the canon numbers throughout Ammonius's four-column synopsis, Eusebius can then add a consecutive enumeration of the sections they create within the text of Matthew. It turns out that there are 355 of them—that is, points where Matthew's relationship with the other gospels changes.[24] In table 5.4, the difference between the section numbers and the canon numbers is represented by Arabic and Roman numerals, respectively. Eusebius himself used black ink for the one, red for the other.

24. The exact demarcation and the enumeration of the sections was almost certainly the work of Eusebius, who needed the numbers for his canon tables, rather than of Ammonius, who did not. "Ammonian sections" or "Ammonian numbers" are therefore misnomers. See Nestle, "Die Eusebianische Evangelien-Synopse," 41. This persistent misunderstanding of Ammonius's work may derive from Jerome, *On Famous Men* 55.

Table 5.4. Addition of Section Numbers (Matthew only)

Matthew 5:1–6	Mark	Luke 6:20–21	John
24 X And seeing the crowds he went up into the mountain, and when he sat down his disciples came to him.			
25 V And opening his mouth he taught them, saying: "Blessed are the poor in spirit, for theirs is the kingdom of heaven.		V And lifting up his eyes to the disciples, he said: "Blessed are the poor, for yours is the kingdom of God.	
26 X "Blessed are the meek, for they shall inherit the earth.			
27 V "Blessed are those who mourn, for they shall be comforted.		<V "Blessed are those who weep now, for you shall laugh.>	
28 V "Blessed are those who hunger and thirst for righteousness, for they shall be satisfied."		V "Blessed are those who hunger now, for you shall be satisfied."	

4. In contrast to Matthew, the Ammonian text of Luke (and Mark and John) is out of sequence, making consecutive section enumeration impossible at this stage. Eusebius must therefore transfer the canon numbers (I–X) into separate texts of the non-Matthean gospels (table 5.5). The textual units created by the canon numbers have all been clearly marked out, and identifying them within their original Lukan, Markan, or Johannine contexts would not be a difficult operation.

Table 5.5. Transfer of Canon Numbers to Luke (Separate Text)

V And lifting up his eyes to the disciples, he said: "Blessed are the poor, for yours is the kingdom of God.
V "Blessed are those who hunger now, for you shall be satisfied.
V "Blessed are those who weep now, for you shall laugh."

5. Once the canon numbers have been transferred to correctly sequenced texts of Mark, Luke, and John, consecutive enumeration of

the resulting sections can be carried out (table 5.6). There prove to be 233 of them in Mark, 342 in Luke, and 232 in John. As in the case of Matthew, the Eusebian sections represent points where there is a change in the relationship of one gospel to the others.

**Table 5.6. Addition of Section Numbers
to Luke (Separate Text)**

---

46 V And lifting up his eyes to the disciples, he said: "Blessed are the poor, for yours is the kingdom of God.
47 V "Blessed are those who hunger now, for you shall be satisfied.
48 V "Blessed are those who weep now, for you shall laugh."

---

6. It is now possible to draw up a set of ten tables (i.e., coordinated lists) and to insert the section numbers for each of the relevant gospels in parallel columns (table 5.7). For example, Matthew's blessing on those who hunger and thirst for righteousness has been enumerated as section 25, and Luke's similar blessing on those who hunger now as section 46. These two figures are therefore found opposite each other in the two columns of canon table V. Information dispersed throughout the gospel texts, in the form of canon and section numbers, is now collected, systematized, and made usable as a cross-referencing system. The figures 25 V in the text of Matthew alert the reader to the existence of a Lukan parallel to the Matthean beatitude, the location of which may be found by consulting canon table V near the beginning of the volume.

**Table 5.7. Transcription
of Enumeration from Texts
to Tables**

Canon V		Canon X$_1$
Matthew	Luke	Matthew
. . .	. . .	. . .
25	46	24
27	48	26
28	47	29

Eusebius's analysis of gospel relationships serves not only as a cross-referencing system but also as a demonstration that a rational order underlies the apparent chaos of gospel interrelations. The two functions are closely related. Cross-referencing may serve not just to satisfy idle curiosity but also to bring that underlying order to light in concrete cases, showing how one gospel passage is enhanced and enriched by comparison with the parallel passages elsewhere. Unlike the modern scholarly "synoptic problem," Eusebius's system does not depend on hypotheses, although it does require interpretative decisions about what counts as a parallel and what does not.

This analysis of gospel parallels is designed for inclusion within a four-gospel codex. Indeed, it cannot exist outside a four-gospel codex, requiring the presence of all four gospels with their section and canon numbers installed at the appropriate places in the margins. In making explicit the connections between one gospel and another, the system also ensures that the four of them are all bound within the covers of a single volume. While that was not in itself an innovation, the norm was for gospels to circulate individually. A fifth-century mosaic from Ravenna still shows four separate books on the upper and lower shelves of an open book-cupboard, Mark and Luke above, Matthew and John below: an apostolic foundation with two postapostolic supplements.[25] Without the Eusebian apparatus, a four-gospel codex would be experienced by its users as no more than the sum of the four individual volumes. The difference between the two formats would go no deeper than the cover and the binding. At most, a link might be inserted between the ending of one gospel and the beginning of another: "Here ends the Gospel according to Matthew. Here begins the Gospel according to Mark." With Eusebius's tables and section enumerations in place, however, around four hundred invisible lines are threaded through the volume, linking almost every page with one, two, or three pages from other gospels, binding them

25. On this mosaic image in the Galla Placidia Mausoleum, Ravenna, see F. Watson, *Gospel Writing*, 577–83, and the accompanying website (https://gospelwriting .wordpress.com/).

tightly together in an intricate network and demonstrating that the single set of covers around the four distinct books is more than just a matter of convenience.

Some four-gospel codices were already in circulation during the third century, but Eusebius was responsible for the first four-gospel *edition*. In the same way, over a century earlier, Irenaeus was the first to define a four-gospel *collection*. If the one and only gospel exists in a fourfold form, then it makes sense to incorporate all four versions of the gospel within a single book—a book that includes a detailed analysis of their interrelatedness, revealing the complex yet harmonious order underlying the apparent chaos of texts that tell the same story so differently. Eusebius's enumeration invites the reader to consult parallel passages in other gospels, comparing and contrasting what is read in one text with what may be read elsewhere. One reads *through* the text, from the beginning toward the end, but one may also now read *across* the text, from one location to a second and perhaps also to a third and fourth. Eusebius's canons bring to light new possibilities for a canonical reading of the fourfold gospel, one that highlights not only its diversity but also its coherence.

If gospel beginnings are a point from which to reflect on diversity, the coherence of the gospels stands out most clearly in their endings. As Jesus arrives in Jerusalem, where he is to suffer, die, and rise again, all four gospels converge. We must look more closely at that convergence, taking Eusebius as our guide.

6

The City and the Garden

"From then on, Jesus began to show his disciples that he must go to Jerusalem and suffer many things from the elders and chief priests and scribes, and be killed and on the third day be raised."[1] Thus the First Evangelist (the first in the canonical collection, not the first to write). The end of Jesus' story casts its shadow far back into the gospel narrative, for the sequence of future events has been scripted in advance within the divine will—as the word "must" indicates. The coming events are "shown" to the disciples, as though set before their eyes as well as addressed to their ears.

Each of the first three evangelists has three different versions of Jesus' prediction of his suffering, death, and resurrection. In Eusebian terms, these passages belong within canon II. As we shall see, there are Johannine equivalents, but they are too dissimilar in placement and wording to qualify for canon I, the list of passages common to all four gospels. In the first passion prediction, only Matthew makes the obvious but necessary point that Jesus must "go to Jerusalem" if his death and resurrection are to come to pass. In the rendering shared

1. Matt. 16:21.

by Mark and Luke, it is said that Jesus is to "suffer many things *and be rejected by* the elders, chief priests and scribes, and be killed."[2] The addition of "and be rejected" turns "suffer many things" into a comprehensive expression covering not only rejection by the Judean authorities but also the whole train of events leading to Jesus' death. The narrative here summarized in advance is rightly described as a "passion narrative," a narrative that recounts Jesus' *passio*, his "suffering." Luke in particular likes to use the verb *paschein* ("suffer") in a comprehensive sense. "Was it not necessary," asks Luke's risen Jesus as he accompanies two unsighted disciples on the road to Emmaus, "for the Christ *to suffer these things* and to enter his glory?"[3] Luke's Last Supper narrative opens by exploiting the coincidental similarity of the Aramaic-derived word for "passover" and the Greek word for "suffering." As his disciples recline at table, Jesus says, "I have eagerly desired to eat this passover [*pascha*] with you before I suffer [*paschein/pathein*]."[4]

In the second and third passion predictions, other events and other terminology come to the fore. We learn that the Son of man must be "handed over" (or "delivered" or "betrayed") to the Jerusalem authorities—obviously with reference to Judas Iscariot. The authorities will "condemn" him and "hand him over" (again) to the gentiles, who will "mock" and "scourge" him before putting him to death.[5] Here too there are differences. Matthew alone specifies the mode of death: it will be by crucifixion.[6] Mark adds a reference to spitting, to which Luke in turn adds a more general reference to mistreatment.[7] In each case a sequence of verbs anticipates a train of events, but in no case are the verbs or events exactly the same. These sequences all culminate in death and resurrection, but they reach that goal by varied routes, each time highlighting different events.

2. Mark 8:31; Luke 9:22.
3. Luke 24:26.
4. Luke 22:15.
5. Matt. 20:18–19; Mark 10:33–34; Luke 18:31–32.
6. Matt. 20:19.
7. Mark 10:34; Luke 18:32.

If we look elsewhere for similar summaries, the differences continue to accumulate. According to Paul, the gospel message is summed up in the claims that Christ died for our sins, that he was buried, that he was raised on the third day, and that he appeared to individuals—Cephas, James, Paul himself—and to smaller or larger groups.[8] In the synoptic passion-and-resurrection predictions, Jesus never mentions his burial or post-Easter appearances. Later, the Apostles' Creed retraces the path from suffering to resurrection, again with significantly different terminology. Jesus Christ "suffered under Pontius Pilate" (*passus sub Pontio Pilato*), a reference to the indignities endured by Jesus in connection with his Roman trial, especially the mockery, spitting, and violence inflicted by Pilate's soldiers. Jesus was "crucified, dead, and buried" (*crucifixus, mortuus, et sepultus*). With the one Matthean exception, the gospel passages prefer to say that Jesus is to be "killed" rather than "crucified." While the Creed's reference to burial echoes Paul, none of the New Testament summaries bracket the resurrection on the third day with a descent into hell and an ascent into heaven. In each of these instances, however, Jesus' death and resurrection are embedded in a longer sequence of events that establishes a specific and unrepeatable narrative context.

No such sequence is anticipated by the Fourth Evangelist. The individual events of the passion are all compressed into the concept of Jesus' "hour," in which even basic distinctions between suffering, death, and resurrection are erased. As early in the narrative as the wedding at Cana, and at an apparently inopportune moment, Jesus tells his mother, "My hour has not yet come."[9] The announcement that "the hour has come for the Son of man to be glorified"[10] occurs in the aftermath of Jesus' triumphal entry into Jerusalem, indicating that everything that takes place from this point to the end of the gospel belongs to the "hour" and the process of glorification. Events unfold in temporal sequence in the Johannine passion

8. 1 Cor. 15:3–8.
9. John 2:4.
10. John 12:23.

narrative just as in the other gospels, but the time they take is that of the appointed hour.

In this chapter and the next, events will be selected from the full passion-and-resurrection sequence in the hope that what the evangelists are striving to communicate will come to light as their texts are read alongside one another. In the present chapter, we will focus on Jesus' entry into Jerusalem and the scene in the garden of Gethsemane; in the next, the crucifixion and the discovery of the empty tomb.

Acclamation

In the Eusebian analysis of a shared gospel story, the vertical column of text is cut into horizontal slices representing the shifting relationships between the evangelists. Even if all four evangelists tell the same story, they do not tell it in the same way. Everywhere there will be variations, omissions, or additions, so that the story is always the story *according to*—as told by—Matthew or Mark or Luke or John. If one story occurs in four versions, however, these are still versions of the same story. In Eusebian terms, the core of the story belongs to canon I, in which passages common to all four evangelists are listed. That is the case with the story of Jesus' "triumphal entry" into Jerusalem, which opens the gospel account of the final days of Jesus' life. At the heart of this story is the acclamation of Jesus by the crowds, described in similar terms by all four evangelists, although supplementary material is variously provided by one or more of them. If, following Eusebius, we derive the basic template from Matthew, the one story in its four versions may be analyzed as illustrated in table 6.1. (An asterisk indicates a passage belonging to a different context with a parallel here in another gospel.)

Read vertically, the individual columns outline the contents of each of the four accounts, although not necessarily in the correct sequence. On its own terms, each version is complete. The reader of Mark or Luke does not encounter an obvious gap in the text at the points where Matthew and John present Jesus' entry into Jerusalem

Table 6.1

Eusebian Canon/Theme	Matthew	Mark	Luke	John
II Instructions: fetching the ass	206 / 21:1–3	117 / 11:1–3	232 / 19:28–31	
VII Fulfillment of Scripture	207 / 21:4–5			101 / 12:14–15
II The ass is brought	208 / 21:6–7	118 / 11:4–7	233 / 19:32–35	
I Acclamation by the crowd	209 / 21:8–9	119 / 11:8–10	234 / 19:36–38	100 / 12:12–13
V Objection of the rulers	*213 / 21:15–16		235 / 19:39–40	
X₃ Weeping over Jerusalem			236 / 19:41–43	
II Jerusalem's fate	*242 / 24:1–2	*137 / 13:1–2	237 / 19:44	
X₄ The event recollected/the Lazarus link/the Greeks				102 / 12:16–22

as the fulfillment of scriptural prophecy. The reader of John has no cause for complaint when informed simply that "Jesus found an ass and sat upon it," without the synoptic explanation as to how the ass was obtained.[11]

Eusebius's analysis does not track every difference. Within the synoptic passage about the finding of the ass, Mark and Luke note—but Matthew does not—that two disciples were instructed to find a "colt . . . on which no one had ever yet sat."[12] This detail has a scriptural background, although neither evangelist draws attention to it. In the prophecy from Zechariah about a kingly arrival in Jerusalem, it is said that the king will come "humble and mounted on an ass and a new colt."[13] Mark—or his source—assumes that the "new colt" has never before been ridden; it has not yet been broken

11. John 12:14.
12. Mark 11:2; Luke 19:30.
13. Zech. 9:9 LXX.

in, so that Jesus' ability to ride it without difficulty is nothing short of miraculous. The colt is commandeered with imperious messianic authority ("The Lord has need of it!"),[14] and that same authority is exercised over the animal itself. In principle the added Markan and Lukan detail might have been assigned to Eusebius's canon VIII, in which thirteen passages common to these two evangelists are listed. Yet his analysis does not keep track of every detail. By encouraging readers to consult parallel passages, Eusebius's canon tables enable them to identify for themselves the differences within the parallels.

Mounted on the ass (and/or on the ass's colt), Jesus rides toward Jerusalem and is acclaimed as the one who comes in the name of the Lord. In the synoptic gospels the crowds process with Jesus toward the city, laying garments and branches on the road in front of him. In John, Jesus is acclaimed by pilgrims who have already arrived in Jerusalem for Passover and who come out of the city to greet him, waving palm branches.[15] The evangelists report their acclamations in similar language:

> *Matthew*: "Hosanna to the son of David, blessed is he who comes in the name of the Lord, hosanna in the highest!"
>
> *Mark*: "Hosanna, blessed is he who comes in the name of the Lord, blessed is the coming kingdom of our father David, hosanna in the highest!"
>
> *Luke*: "Blessed is the king who comes in the name of the Lord, peace in heaven and glory in the highest!"
>
> *John*: "Hosanna, blessed is he who comes in the name of the Lord, the king of Israel!"[16]

"Hosanna" is *hôšîāh-nā*, a plea for salvation drawn from Psalm 118 and immediately preceding the blessing of the one who comes in

---

14. Mark 11:3.
15. Matt. 21:8; Mark 11:7–8; Luke 19:36 (garments only); John 12:13.
16. Matt. 21:9; Mark 11:9–10; Luke 19:38; John 12:13.

the name of the Lord.[17] Here the phrase has lost its original Hebrew meaning and seems roughly equivalent to "Alleluia" or (as Luke notes) "Glory."

The psalm also poses a more significant problem. In addition to its pleas or acclamations, it also speaks of a mysterious "stone":

> The stone which the builders rejected has become the head of the corner. This is from the LORD, and it is wonderful in our eyes. This is the day that the LORD made—let us rejoice and be glad in it. O LORD, save! O LORD, make us prosper! Blessed is he who comes in the name of the LORD, we bless you from the house of the LORD![18]

Early Christians found in the stone saying an important scriptural testimony to the death and resurrection of Jesus. When Mark and Luke have Jesus speak of being "rejected" by the Jerusalem authorities, the rejected-stone passage is already in mind.[19] It comes fully into view when Jesus quotes it at the conclusion of his parable of the wicked tenants. What, Jesus asks his audience, will the vineyard owner do to tenants who have treated his servants so outrageously and put his own son to death?

> They said to him, "He will utterly destroy those wicked people and will give the vineyard to other tenants." Jesus said to them, "Have you never read in the scriptures, 'The stone which the builders rejected has become the head of the corner. This is from the Lord, and it is wonderful in our eyes'?"[20]

Here, as in the passion predictions, Jesus anticipates the rejection and vindication that are imminent but have not yet taken place. At this point a problem comes to light that goes to the heart of the triumphal-entry story. In the psalm, the acclamation of the one who comes in the name of the Lord *follows* the vindication of the rejected

17. Ps. 118:25–26a.
18. Ps. 117[118]:22–26 LXX.
19. Mark 8:31; Luke 9:22.
20. Matt. 21:41–42; cf. Mark 12:10; Luke 20:16–17.

stone. In the gospels, the acclamation *precedes* both the rejection
and the vindication. It is utterly premature. Jesus rides toward the
holy city in kingly majesty, and he is acclaimed with extravagant
enthusiasm—but within a few days he will be publicly and shame-
fully executed. The first Palm Sunday procession seems to be based
on false hopes. In Mark and still more clearly in Matthew, Jesus
is acknowledged as a Davidic Messiah; he remains a kingly figure
in Luke and John.[21] Yet he himself will shortly cast doubt on the
Messiah's Davidic credentials: "If David calls him 'Lord,' how is
he his son?"[22] So much for the crowds with their "Hosanna to the
son of David!" Above all, it is as "king of the Jews" that Jesus will
be crucified.[23] The Palm Sunday story, so reassuringly familiar, is
at odds with its own narrative context. The problem posed by the
psalm—with its sequence of rejection, vindication, and only then
acclamation—is writ large across the narrative of all four gospels,
in which acclamation comes first and is followed by rejection. There
is no hint of criticism of those who strew garments or branches on
the road to honor the son of David. In none of these accounts does
Jesus dissociate himself from the crowds' enthusiasm, as he does in
the Johannine version of the feeding of the five thousand, in which
he escapes into the solitude of the mountains rather than accede to
the popular demand for him to be made king.[24] Why does he now
appear to accept the kingship that he earlier rejected, although he is
fully aware of the fate that awaits him in Jerusalem? Between them,
the evangelists suggest several answers to this question.

Reading the Event

According to Matthew, Jesus stages this messianic demonstration in
order to fulfill the prophecy of Zechariah:

21. Matt. 21:9; Mark 11:10; Luke 19:38; John 12:13.
22. Matt. 22:45; cf. Mark 12:37; Luke 20:44.
23. Matt. 27:37; Mark 15:26; Luke 23:38; John 19:19–22.
24. John 6:15.

> This took place to fulfill what was said by the prophet: "Say to the daughter of Zion, behold, your king comes to you, gentle and mounted on an ass and on a colt the foal of an ass."[25]

The demonstration is an announcement or proclamation. "Say to the daughter of Zion" is derived from Isaiah 62:11; it replaces the exhortation to "rejoice greatly, O daughter of Zion" in the Zechariah passage. The First Evangelist has been much derided for having Jesus ride on two animals at once, although that is exactly what the prophetic passage appears to say: the king will arrive "righteous and bringing salvation, gentle and mounted on an ass and a new colt."[26] More significant than Matthew's inclusion of both animals is his omission of the kingly attributes of righteousness and salvation so as to place all the emphasis on "gentle" (*praus*). In context this must be a regal gentleness, although gentleness is not normally characteristic of kings approaching a city where their authority is unrecognized. Unlike other kings, the one who comes in the name of the Lord does not issue threats of massacre and destruction. Even the violence in the temple that is shortly to follow is purely symbolic. For Matthew, the messianic demonstration announces to the daughter of Zion the coming of a king who intends not harm but only good.

In Mark's rendering of the story, the scriptural background is never made explicit, and the reasons for Jesus' action are left in obscurity.[27] He is fulfilling his divinely intended destiny, which is to go to Jerusalem to suffer and die, and—so the reader must assume—the manner of his arrival there is all part of the divine plan. What happens is what has to happen. The distinctive Markan secrecy theme may be relevant here. Jesus arrives in Jerusalem at the end of the southward journey that began in Caesarea Philippi, where he imposed strict secrecy about his identity as the Christ, confessed by Peter.[28] He traveled incognito:

25. Matt. 21:4–5, citing Zech. 9:9.
26. Zech. 9:9 LXX.
27. Mark's text is full of intertextual echoes of Scripture, but the evangelist rarely makes his use of Scripture explicit. On this see R. Hays, *Reading Backwards*, 17–33.
28. Mark 8:27–30.

he "passed through Galilee, and did not want anyone to know."[29] As he approaches his journey's end, however, he is loudly and insistently proclaimed as "son of David" by blind Bartimaeus and, immediately afterward, as the messianic restorer of David's kingdom by the festival crowds.[30] In the second instance, Jesus actively provokes the messianic demonstration by his arrival in royal majesty, thus initiating the train of events that leads to his death as the "Christ, the king of Israel" or as "the king of the Jews."[31] It is Jesus' public acclamation as Messiah that enables the authorities to frame plausible charges against him.

Luke offers a very different and more explicit interpretation of this paradoxical story in his two contrasting additions to it:

> As he was now drawing near to the descent of the Mount of Olives, the whole crowd of disciples began to rejoice and praise God with a loud voice for all the mighty works they had seen, saying, "Blessed is the King who comes in the name of the Lord."[32]

> And as he drew near and saw the city, he wept over it, saying, "If only you knew this day the things that make for peace! But now they are hidden from your eyes. For days will come upon you when your enemies will cast up a bank against you and besiege you and oppress you on every side, and dash you and your children within you to the ground, and they will not leave one stone upon another within you, because you did not know the time of your visitation."[33]

Although Jesus is acclaimed as king as in the other gospel accounts, this evangelist sees the crowds as responding retrospectively to his activity as a worker of signs and wonders, of which they were eyewitnesses. Luke's pilgrims are Galileans who have seen for themselves how, through Jesus' ministry, "the blind receive their sight, the lame walk, lepers are cleansed, the deaf hear, [and] the dead are raised

29. Mark 9:30.
30. Mark 10:47–48; 11:10.
31. Mark 15:26, 32; cf. 14:61–62.
32. Luke 19:37–38.
33. Luke 19:41–44.

up."[34] From this point on there will be no further healings, with the exception of a severed ear in the garden of Gethsemane,[35] and—for Luke—this is the right moment to celebrate the phase of Jesus' ministry that is now completed. But if there is a past to celebrate, there is also a future, known only to Jesus, that causes him to weep. Later, on his way to the cross, the Lukan Jesus will warn the daughters of Jerusalem to weep not for him but for themselves.[36] He himself does likewise when he first catches sight of the holy city and sees it not only as it is but also as it will be in the days when it becomes the site of unimaginable acts of violence.

For John, as for Luke, the triumphal entry is associated with Jesus' miracle-working powers. The Johannine crowd bears witness not only to Jesus as the king of Israel but also to his raising Lazarus from the dead—a single, unique, recent miracle in nearby Bethany rather than a general pattern of activity in distant Galilee.[37] While the Zechariah connection is duly noted, as in Matthew, here there is a surprising twist:

> And Jesus found a young ass and sat upon it, as it is written: "Fear not, daughter of Jerusalem, behold your king comes, seated upon an ass's foal." The disciples did not understand at first, but when Jesus was glorified, *then* they remembered that all this was written about him and happened to him.[38]

A slippage occurs here between the event as perceived at the time and the same event seen in retrospect. At the time, the disciples were immersed in the event as it unfolded. For the duration of this scene they are merged into the crowd, no doubt participating in its hosannas. Yet, according to the narrator, they lacked any understanding of the event's true significance. Whatever they thought at

34. Luke 7:22.
35. Luke 22:50–51.
36. Luke 23:28.
37. Cf. John 12:13–19.
38. John 12:14–16.

the time has proved to be mistaken, misguided, or otherwise irrelevant. Only later did they learn to make scriptural sense of Jesus'
arrival in Jerusalem, reconfiguring it around the key scriptural text
(Zech. 9:9) that had meanwhile come to mind. Yet the event cannot
be understood on the basis of purely scriptural resources. It must be
seen in light of the greater event to which it belongs, that of Jesus'
glorification—his enthronement in heavenly glory, accomplished
not only in his resurrection and ascension but also in his crucifixion. As it refers back to the prophetic text, Jesus' acclamation
also points ahead to his true enthronement, of which it is a sign or
parable.

The four versions of the story share a common core. In Eusebian
terms, it belongs to canon I. The evangelists' interpretations of that
common core take them in different directions, although significant
convergences between two or three of them can still be traced. In
their combined testimony they speak of Jesus' momentous arrival in
Jerusalem as an *open* event that provokes reflection rather than bearing its meaning on its surface—but as a distinct *event* nevertheless,
with its own unique contours and context.

A Man of Sorrows

The gospel passion narratives consist of a sequence of interconnected
episodes. Each has its own place in the sequence. Unlike the evangelists' accounts of Jesus' miracles and controversies, the order of
the episodes cannot be significantly varied. Yet each episode is also
complete in itself, offering its own unique perspective on the total event
that Luke earlier described as "the exodus that Jesus was to fulfill in
Jerusalem."[39] If the accounts of his arrival in Jerusalem present that
exodus as a triumph or victory, the Gethsemane episode points to its
human cost: suffering and abandonment. Here too there are multiple
versions—four of them, according to Eusebius, although the fourth

39. Luke 9:31.

exists only in fragments that must be reassembled from various points in the Johannine narrative (see table 6.2).

Table 6.2

Eusebian Canon/ Theme	Matthew	Mark	Luke	John
I Gethsemane	291 / 26:36a	172 / 14:32a	279 / 22:39	156 / 18:1
VI "Sit while I pray"	292 / 26:36b–37	173 / 14:32b–33		
IV Jesus' sorrow	293 / 26:38	174 / 14:34		107 / 12:27a
I Prayer, cup	294 / 26:39a	175 / 14:35–36a	281 / 22:41–42a	161 / 18:11b
I "Not my will . . ."	295 / 26:39b	176 / 14:36b	282 / 22:42b	42 / 5:30b
II Exhortation to pray	296 / 26:40–41a	177 / 14:37–38a	280 / 22:40	
X_3 The angel and the agony			283 / 22:43–44	
II Exhortation to pray	296 / 26:40–41a	177 / 14:37–38a	284 / 22:45–46	
IV Spirit and flesh	297 / 26:41b	178 / 14:38b		70 / 6:63a
VI Disciples sleep again	298 / 26:42–44	179 / 14:39–40		
IV The hour has come	299 / 26:45–46	180 / 14:41–42		103 / 12:23

Eusebius's analysis shows that the relationship between the first three accounts is relatively straightforward. Matthew and Mark keep pace with each other. There is no obvious difference in order or content, although here as always small-scale variations come to light on closer inspection of the parallel passages. The repetition of one pair of section numbers (Matthew *296*, Mark *177*) is occasioned by the fact that the exhortation to "pray that you may not enter into temptation" occurs twice in Luke, at the beginning and the end of this episode (Luke *280*, *284*). As always, the section enumeration in one gospel is determined by what is happening in the others, and this is true also of the repetitions that are a regular feature of Eusebius's tables. For the same reason, the numerical sequence in the Luke column (*279–281–282–280–283–284*) reflects a transposition necessary in order to display the parallels with Matthew and Mark. Eusebius's Luke text includes the account of Jesus' agony, absent from many ancient manuscripts.[40] Being unique to Luke, this is assigned to canon X.

In the John column, the sequence *156–107–161–42–70–103* contains only two sections (*156, 161*) that belong to the Johannine Gethsemane account, in which there is no mention of Jesus' prayer or the disciples' failure to pray. Four more sections have been gathered together from elsewhere. The Johannine sequence represents the following set of parallels to the synoptic versions of this episode:

156 I: After saying these things, Jesus went out with his disciples across the brook Kidron, where there was a garden into which he entered with his disciples.[41]

107 IV: "Now is my soul troubled, and what shall I say? Father, save me from this hour."[42]

161 I: "The cup which the Father gave me, shall I not drink it?"[43]

42 I: "I seek not my own will but the will of the one who sent me."[44]

70 IV: "It is the Spirit that gives life, the flesh can achieve nothing."[45]

103 IV: And Jesus answered them, saying, "The hour has come for the Son of man to be glorified."[46]

40. The Greek textual evidence is well set out by R. Swanson, *New Testament Greek Manuscripts: Luke*, 375–76. See also B. Metzger, *Textual Commentary*, 177.
41. John 18:1.
42. John 12:27a.
43. John 18:11b.
44. John 5:30b.
45. John 6:63a.
46. John 12:23.

Identifying these scattered Johannine parallels to the synoptic Gethsemane story is a significant scholarly achievement, for which Eusebius is presumably indebted to his predecessor Ammonius of Alexandria. These passages were probably already present in the John column of Ammonius's gospel synopsis, opposite the Gethsemane episode in the first three columns. Sections *107* and *103* occur within the extended Johannine account of the triumphal entry and its aftermath, suggesting hidden affinities between the two very different episodes. What Jesus says, does, and experiences in Gethsemane is in keeping with what he says, does, and experiences elsewhere. Already as he enters Jerusalem his soul is troubled because his hour has come. In submitting his will to the Father's in Gethsemane, he does in new and unprecedented circumstances what he has always done.

The character of Luke's version of this episode depends on whether the unique account of Jesus' agony is included or excluded. From a text-critical standpoint, the evidence suggests an early addition to the text rather than composition by the Third Evangelist. From a canonical standpoint, it seems preferable to accept the undeniable reality that the text of Luke's Gethsemane account circulated from early in its history in two forms, one longer and one shorter. The further back an interpolation can be traced, the harder it becomes to differentiate it from the other editorial and scribal practices involved in gospel composition. Evangelists themselves are editors as well as authors, and additional editorial activity is a continuation of their work rather than a corruption of it.

In the text as read not only by Eusebius in the fourth century but also by Justin Martyr in the mid-second, the prayer that the cup be taken away is followed by a passage of extraordinary and painful intensity:

> And there appeared to him an angel from heaven, strengthening him. And being in agony he prayed still more fervently, and his sweat became like drops of blood falling upon the ground.[47]

47. Luke 22:43–44.

The appearance of an angel from heaven ought to be reassuring. Even if the disciples sleep, Jesus has not been abandoned. And yet the strength bestowed by this angel is not that of comfort or courage but the ability to endure in prayer, in spite of agony and anxiety accompanied by distressing physical manifestations.[48] In the first two gospels, Jesus confesses to Peter, James, and John, "My soul is very sorrowful, even to death."[49] In the longer Lukan text, the soul's agony is shared by the body. Appropriately or otherwise, Justin connects this passage to Psalm 22 (21 LXX):

> And as for this passage, "Like water all my bones are poured out and dispersed, my heart has become like wax, melting in the midst of my breast," this foreshadows what happened to him on the night when they came to the Mount of Olives to arrest him. For in the Memoirs [*Apomnēmoneumata*], which (as I have said) were composed by his apostles and those who followed them, it states that "sweat poured out like drops" as he prayed saying, "If possible let this cup pass from me." His heart and also his bones trembled, his heart melted like wax in his breast, so that we may realize that the Father willed that his own Son should truly endure such sufferings for our sake, and may *not* say that he, being God's Son, did not feel what happened to him and was done to him.[50]

Here the wording of Jesus' prayer is Matthean rather than Lukan: "If possible, let this cup pass from me" rather than "If you will, remove this cup from me."[51] Justin sees the "Memoirs" as a collective apostolic and postapostolic production and can move freely between Matthew and Luke without differentiating between them. It is almost certainly in his text of Luke that he reads of the great drops of sweat,

48. As Karl Barth notes, the angel's appearance "is not an ending of the necessary conflict brought about from heaven, but, according to the presentation in Luke, the battle in which he is engaged only becomes severe after this strengthening" (*CD* IV/1, 268).
49. Matt. 26:37–38; Mark 14:33–34.
50. Justin Martyr, *Dialogue with Trypho*, 103.7–8, citing Ps. 21:15 LXX.
51. Matt. 26:39; Luke 22:42. Justin omits "Father."

linking them to the psalmist's graphic account of the dissolution and liquefaction of the very structure of the body.

As Justin already recognized, no reader of the longer form of Luke's Gethsemane story could possibly think that, as God's Son, Jesus endured what happened to him with serene indifference. With the shorter text it is another matter. While there is no question here of a "docetic" denial of Jesus' true humanity, this Lukan Jesus is concerned only to teach his disciples a lesson about prayer in time of trial, and he gives no indication of distress on his own account. As soon as they reach the garden, Jesus instructs the disciples to "pray that you enter not into temptation."[52] There is no confession of grief and dismay to an inner circle of three disciples. Jesus' exemplary prayer is for the removal of the cup but above all for the fulfillment of God's will, and that is just the prayer that the disciples too should be praying. In fact they are asleep—not from negligence but, as Luke tells us, from sheer grief.[53] So Jesus wakes them and repeats the instruction to "pray that you enter not into temptation."[54] As he is speaking, however, Judas arrives with the arresting party.[55] The opportunity for prayer has passed. Jesus has availed himself of that opportunity and endures the trials that follow with exemplary fortitude. Peter, his negative counterpart, has failed to pray and will shortly deny Jesus three times.

In the shorter Lukan account and its supplement, two possible approaches to this story are illustrated. The story can be presented as exemplary. Christians, called to imitate Jesus, should learn from his conduct in Gethsemane how they are to face their own times of trial. They are to pray for deliverance while subordinating their own natural human instinct of self-preservation to the will of God—the God who is not some harsh impersonal fate but who may confidently be addressed as "Father." Additionally or alternatively, the story can be presented as part of Jesus' unique biography. That is where the

52. Luke 22:40.
53. Luke 22:45.
54. Luke 22:46.
55. Luke 22:47.

emphasis lies in the longer text. There is nothing exemplary about
the angelic visitation, the agony, or the sweat-like drops of blood. The
language evokes an abyss of suffering into which Jesus is plunged,
while the reader remains a bystander looking on, appalled and fas-
cinated. Here Jesus' sufferings are exclusively his own. So powerful
is the image of the unique agony that the exemplary significance of
Jesus' prayer will tend to be overlooked. The two Lukan versions of
this story are at odds with each other.

Something of the same tension may be seen in Matthew and Mark.
Initially it is the biographical tendency that predominates. The disciples are instructed not to pray but merely to "sit here while *I* go
over there to pray."[56] In what may be an addition to an earlier and
simpler version of this story, Jesus then takes three named disciples
with him, confesses his distress, and tells them to "remain here and
watch with me."[57] Two groups of disciples are apparently located at
different points in the garden while Jesus proceeds to a third location
in order to begin praying. The concern seems largely biographical. It
is true that Mark in particular has earlier emphasized the importance
of watching, pointedly extending Jesus' exhortation to watch to all
his readers. The eschatological discourse immediately preceding the
passion narrative ends with the words "And what I say to you I say
to all: Watch!"[58] Here, the watching or keeping awake is obviously
metaphorical. In the midst of the strains and stresses of the end times,
Mark's readers are to maintain faith, hope, and patience as they look
for the coming of the Son of man. The metaphor grows naturally out
of a brief parable-like passage in which a doorkeeper is appointed to
keep watch for the master's return at some unpredictable hour of the
day or night.[59] In Gethsemane, however, watching or keeping awake
has to do not with eschatology but with a unique and unrepeatable
occasion in the life of Jesus. "Stay here and watch" (Mark) or "Stay
here and watch with me" (Matthew) is best understood as an urgent

56. Matt. 26:36; cf. Mark 14:32.
57. Matt. 26:37–38; cf. Mark 14:33–34.
58. Mark 13:37.
59. Mark 13:33–37.

request for solidarity at a moment of acute crisis.[60] This is a literal watching, not a metaphorical one.

After his first prayer, Jesus returns to the disciples and finds them asleep. The two groups created by Jesus' confession of his distress have now merged again into one, so that Peter is singled out as the representative not of the inner circle but of the Eleven: "Simon, are you asleep?"[61] It is at this point that a biographically oriented narrative reveals its exemplary dimension:

> Could you not watch with me one hour? Watch and pray that you may not enter into temptation. The spirit is willing, but the flesh is weak.[62]

In the three parts of Jesus' address to Peter, we move from literal wakefulness to a general attitude of spiritual alertness to a still more general explanation of why disciples sometimes fail to act on what they know to be right. This passage provides the cue for Luke's more consistently exemplary treatment of this story, just as the confession of distress provides the cue for the dramatic post-Lukan depiction of the agony of soul and body.

At the end of the story in its Matthean and Markan form, it is clear that the exemplary dimension is secondary to and dependent on the biographical one: "Behold, the hour has come and the Son of man is betrayed into the hands of sinners!"[63] Judas, the betrayer, is not a negative example of generally inappropriate conduct, as Peter is when he neglects to pray and so fails when the moment of testing comes. Judas's act is as unique and unrepeatable as Jesus' agony. Again, it evokes horror and fascination. Yet, aware of Judas's approach, Jesus goes out to meet him: "Rise, let us be going; see, my betrayer is at hand!"[64] In doing so he takes to himself the cup that is held out to him, which he had asked to be spared from but which he

60. Mark 14:34; Matt. 26:38.
61. Mark 14:37.
62. Matt. 26:40–41; cf. Mark 14:37–38.
63. Matt. 26:45; cf. Mark 14:41.
64. Matt. 26:46; Mark 14:42.

now knows he must accept. Thus the Johannine Jesus addresses his disciples: "The cup which the Father gave me, shall I not drink it?"[65] Why is the cup given, and why must its contents be drunk? Because the hour of the Son of man's betrayal is also the hour for the Son of man to be glorified.[66] Jesus was triumphantly acclaimed as king when he arrived in Jerusalem, and—although his disciples did not know it at the time—his royal triumph is manifested in his suffering and death no less than in his resurrection.

65. John 18:11.
66. John 12:23.

7

Christus Victor

Dating back to around the fifth or sixth century, an ancient Ethiopic gospel book preserves what is probably the oldest surviving set of evangelist portraits. The book may have been produced in the Abba Garima monastery in northern Ethiopia, where it remains to this day and after which it is named "Garima III." The monastery itself is located in the midst of spectacular mountain scenery near the site of the Battle of Adwa, at which the Ethiopians achieved a celebrated victory over Italian would-be colonizers in 1896. A few miles farther away lies the city of Aksum, in late antiquity the capital of a flourishing civilization, Christian since the fourth century when the first bishop of Aksum was appointed by no less a person than Athanasius, patriarch of Alexandria and defender of the Nicene faith. The Abba Garima monastery may have enjoyed royal patronage. The gospel book's silver covers and the exceptional quality of its artwork suggest that material resources were not lacking.[1]

1. On the Garima Gospels, see the forthcoming fully illustrated work by J. McKenzie and F. Watson, *Early Illuminated Gospel Books*. The importance of these books was recognized by, among others, J. Leroy, "Un nouvel évangéliaire éthiopien illustré du monastère d'Abba Garima," and A. Bausi, "'True Story' of the Abba Gärima Gospels."

The evangelist portraits are to be found at the beginnings of the corresponding sections of the book—Matthew at the start of the section devoted to his gospel, and so on. One portrait stands out from the others. Mark is portrayed in profile, seated on a chair representing the episcopal throne of Alexandria, which, according to tradition, he was the first to occupy. His gospel book lies in his lap; he is about to place it on the ornamental reading desk that stands in front of him. In the other three portraits the evangelists are depicted as facing the viewer, standing on low platforms that represent their roles as both proclaimers and writers of the gospel. Although dressed differently, they are remarkably similar in appearance. Each of them displays his gospel book, the spine of which rests on his bent left forearm while the elongated first and second fingers of his right hand are extended over the book in a gesture of blessing, commending it to the reader. The book itself is a codex secured with ties, its front cover adorned with a cross. The crosses differ slightly in appearance, but they clearly identify the books themselves as gospels. In a fifth portrait of a figure holding a book, the cross is lacking from the book's front cover, and the parallel lines that replace it indicate that this is Eusebius, author of the canon tables, which are also prominently featured in this volume. The role of Eusebius as editor of the four-gospel codex is differentiated from that of the evangelists, whose calling it is to bear witness to the cross. The cover design of their gospel books is an expression of their common theme: the cross as the place of Christ's costly victory over the powers of darkness.

These evangelist portraits draw attention to what the four evangelists share rather than what differentiates them. Absent here are the evangelist symbols that, in Latin gospel books, emphasize the difference. In the Western books the evangelist symbols point to the gospels' diverse beginnings: the human genealogy, the roar from the wilderness, the temple as the place of sacrifice, the eagle that soars into divine realms.[2] The Ethiopian portraits represent the gospels'

2. The eighth-century Lindisfarne Gospels are a representative example of Western evangelist portraits with symbols. See M. Brown, *Lindisfarne Gospels*, 114–23; R. Gameson, *From Holy Island to Durham*, 57–61.

convergent endings. The crosses on the book covers differ in appearance, for the evangelists do not recount the denouement of Jesus' story in exactly the same way. (Thus John's cross has the Greek letter *chi* superimposed on it, standing for *Christos* and creating an eight-point figure resembling a star.) Yet the emphasis on the gospels' shared conclusion is clear. In each of the four quadrants created by these crosses, oval shapes representing jewels show that the place of shame has become a place of glory. Cross and resurrection belong together as two sides of a single event. The crucifixion is backlit by the radiance of Easter morning.

This view of the cross is also apparent in the gospel books of the Latin West. Surviving parts of one such book are preserved in the library of Durham Cathedral.[3] Dating probably from the latter part of the seventh century, this Northumbrian book may derive from the monastery on the island of Lindisfarne that was to produce the better-known Lindisfarne Gospels a few decades later. The Matthew section of the Durham Gospels closes with a unique depiction of Christ reigning from the cross.[4] To eyes accustomed to later portrayals of Christ's sufferings, his appearance here is utterly unfamiliar and disturbing. He is fully clothed in a long robe. His beard flows down to his chest, where its divided ends match the folds in his robe below. His darkened eyes stare directly at the viewer and contrast with the golden halo whose two ends meet the downward curve of his shoulders. The halo might also be interpreted as Christ's hair, which, according to the book of Revelation, was "white as white wool, white as snow."[5] His head and shoulders are raised well above the horizontal beam of the cross, along which his arms are extended only from the elbows. He appears to be seated, as though enthroned. In the two lower quadrants created by the cross are the soldiers who pierced Jesus' side with a spear thrust and who offered him vinegar on a sponge; the first of these is identified as Longinus. The upper

3. See full bibliographical details in P. McGurk, *Latin Gospel Books*, 29–30. For analysis of the artwork, see J. J. G. Alexander, *Insular Manuscripts*, 40–42.

4. For this image, search online for "Durham Gospels."

5. Rev. 1:14.

quadrants are occupied by two fiery seraphim, their haloed heads a little above Christ's. This crucifixion scene is also Isaiah's vision of the Lord seated upon a throne, high and lifted up, with the six-winged seraphim standing above him.[6]

This crucifixion-enthronement is interpreted by way of a series of inscriptions. Above the figure of Christ stand words familiar from all four gospels: *Hic est Iesus Rex Iudeorum*, "This is Jesus King of the Jews." On either side of his head are the letters A and Ω, *Alpha* and *Omega*, for he is not just an incidental figure within the human story but "the first and the last, the beginning and the end."[7] In the upper margin we read: *Scito quis et qualis est qui talia . . . passus pro nobis . . .* ("Know who and what he is who suffered such things for us"). The Christ who suffers on the cross is also the risen Christ. In the left margin the viewer is directed from Christ's sufferings to his resurrection and ascension in the words of the Apostles' Creed: *Surrexit a mortuis, [sedet ad] dexteram patris* ("He rose from the dead, he sits at the right hand of the Father"). The image depicts the risen and enthroned Christ no less than the Christ who suffers, for these are one and the same. In the right margin the purpose of his sufferings is stated more fully: *Auctorem mortis deiiciens vitam nostram restituens si tamen compatiamur* ("Casting out the author of death, restoring our life, if indeed we suffer with him"). The final phrase is drawn from Paul,[8] but the expulsion of the devil is a Johannine motif: "Now is the judgment of the world, now is the ruler of this world cast out."[9] Reigning from the cross, Christ is victorious over death and all the powers of darkness.

In the Ethiopian evangelist portraits, the cross is the common theme of all four gospels. A similar point is made when the Northumbrian book places the crucifixion image at the close of Matthew's gospel, as if to sum up the essential content it shares with the others.

6. Isa. 6:1–2.
7. Rev. 22:13; cf. 1:8.
8. Rom. 8:17.
9. John 12:31.

Although separated geographically by up to four thousand miles, gospel books of the East and the West have much in common in their format, supplementary material, and artwork. One such common feature is the use of the Eusebian canon tables, an indispensable guide for any reader who wishes to know which passages occur in which gospels.

The Death of the Messiah

The intricate Eusebian analysis of the four canonical accounts of Jesus' death is set out in table 7.1 (pp. 150–51).

Retaining the order common to Matthew and Mark causes significant displacements in Luke and John. The core elements in this four-fold account are represented by the canon I passages and supported by canon II passages omitted only by John. Canon I passages tell of the arrival at Golgotha, the parting of the garments, the placard, the two thieves, and Jesus' death. To this list should be added the vinegar in the sponge; here Eusebius has made one of his rare mistakes by linking the Johannine version of this motif to the earlier offer of wine at the moment of crucifixion (thus John *203* is out of sequence). Another such mistake might be seen in the division of the passages on the women at the cross between canons X_4 (John *202*), VI (Matthew *347*, Mark *226*), and X_3 (Luke *331*). Here, however, unique elements are still present in both canon X passages: the entrusting of Jesus' mother to the beloved disciple in the case of John, the grief of the crowds in the case of Luke. Canon II passages include the mockery of the chief priests and of the thieves, the darkness, the tearing of the temple veil, and the centurion's confession. The absence of these passages from John is consistent with his own distinctive conception of the crucifixion as an act of enthronement, as we shall see. It is notable that, with the partial exception of Luke, the evangelists pass rapidly over the act of crucifixion itself, tending to subordinate it to the parting of the garments.

Table 7.1

Eusebian Canon/ Theme	Matthew	Mark	Luke	John
I Arrival at Golgotha	332 / 27:33	210 / 15:22	318 / 23:33a	197 / 19:17–18a
IV The offer of wine	333 / 27:34	211 / 15:23		203 / 19:28–30
I The parting of the garments	334 / 27:35–36	212 / 15:24	321 / 23:34b	201 / 19:23–24
X₄ Women at the cross (1)				202 / 19:25–27
X₂ The third hour		213 / 15:25		
I The placard	335 / 27:37	214 / 15:26	324 / 23:38	199 / 19:19
X₄ "What I have written . . ."				200 / 19:20–22
X₃ "Father, forgive . . ."			320 / 23:34a	
I The two criminals	336 / 27:38	215 / 15:27a	317 / 23:32	198 / 19:18b
	336 / 27:38	215 / 15:27a	319 / 23:33b	198 / 19:18b
VIII Reckoned with the lawless		216 / 15:27b–28	*277 / 22:37	
VI Mockery of the passers-by	337 / 27:39–40	217 / 15:29–30		
II Mockery of the chief priests	338 / 27:41–43	218 / 15:31–32a	322 / 23:35	
II Mockery of the thieves	339 / 27:44	219 / 15:32b	325 / 23:39	
X₃ The penitent thief			326 / 23:40–42	
II The darkness	340 / 27:45	220 / 15:33	327 / 23:44–45a	
VI "My God, my God . . ."	341 / 27:46–47	221 / 15:34–35		
II Vinegar in a sponge	342 / 27:48–49	222 / 15:36	323 / 23:36	

Eusebian Canon/ Theme	Matthew	Mark	Luke	John
I The death of Jesus	343 / 27:50	223 / 15:37	329 / 23:46	204 / 19:30
II The veil	344 / 27:51a	224 / 15:38	328 / 23:45b	
X₁ The earthquake	345 / 27:51b–53			
II Centurion's confession	346 / 27:54	225 / 15:39	330 / 23:47	
VI Women at the cross (2)	347 / 27:55–56	226 / 15:40–41		
X₃ The crowds and the witnesses			331 / 23:48–49	
X₄ The piercing				205 / 19:31–37

Each gospel has at least one passage in the canon X category, and in every case the distinctive passage has its origins in the shared canon I or II passage to which it is attached. To the common reference to the act of crucifixion, Mark adds a note about the time of day,[10] while Luke attaches the saying "Father, forgive them, for they know not what they do."[11] The reference to the two thieves crucified with Jesus, one on his right and the other on his left, is the starting point for Luke's account of the penitent thief. John develops the traditional motifs of the placard and the women at the cross; Matthew associates the tearing of the temple veil with an earthquake and the resurrection of the saints. A further canon X passage might have been extracted from Luke 23:46, where the "loud cry" with which Jesus died becomes articulate in the words "Father, into your hands I commit my spirit."

In spite of its shortcomings, Eusebius's analysis sets out the formal relationships between the gospel accounts clearly and effectively. It

10. Mark 15:25.
11. Luke 23:34.

lays a foundation on which to build an interpretation of the event that constitutes the goal of the entire gospel narrative. As the combination of canons I, II, and X passages already suggests, the various gospel accounts offer different angles on a sequence of events they share with one another. In Matthew and in Mark, Jesus dies on behalf of others and as their substitute. In Luke, the manner of Jesus' death provides a pattern for his followers to imitate. In John, Jesus' crucifixion is his paradoxical enthronement as king and the supreme revelation of his glory as the source of eternal life. These perspectives on Jesus' death provide the framework for the discussions that follow.

Atonement

Like some other ancient modes of punishment, crucifixion was staged as a spectacle that exposed the victim to public contempt. This harsh reality is reflected in the first three gospels, in which Eusebius's section numbers differentiate three episodes of mockery. In the first of these, present only in Matthew and Mark and so belonging to canon VI, it is the "passers-by" who taunt Jesus for his alleged threat to the temple: "You who would destroy the temple and build it in three days, save yourself, if you are the Son of God, and come down from the cross!"[12] The taunt echoes the accusation made by "false witnesses" at Jesus' trial before the Sanhedrin during the previous night.[13] In the second episode, Jesus is mocked by a group of chief priests, scribes, and elders (Matthew), chief priests and scribes (Mark), or "rulers" (Luke).[14] Of the three versions of their taunts, the shortest is provided by Luke, the longest by Matthew:

> *Luke*: "He saved others, let him save himself, if this is the Christ of God, the Chosen One!"[15]

12. Matt. 27:39–40; cf. Mark 15:29–30, in which the phrase "if you are the Son of God" is lacking.
13. Matt. 26:61; Mark 14:58.
14. Matt. 27:41–43; Mark 15:31–32; Luke 23:35.
15. Luke 23:35.

Mark: "He saved others, himself he cannot save! Let the Christ the king of Israel come down now from the cross so that we may see and believe!"[16]

Matthew: "He saved others, himself he cannot save! He is the king of Israel—let him come down now from the cross and we will believe in him! He trusted in God—let him deliver him now, if he delights in him! For he said, 'I am the Son of God!'"[17]

In a brief third mockery episode, the two condemned criminals join in the general hostility toward Jesus, although in Luke one of them speaks in his defense.[18]

It is the second episode that carries the most weight. Common to all three versions are the words "He saved others, himself he cannot save" (with "he cannot save" replaced by "let him save" in Luke). Intended as a taunt, these words are understood by the evangelists as an unintended statement of the truth. Jesus did indeed save others while unable to save himself—"unable" in the sense that he was unwilling to disregard his Father's will, as the Gethsemane story indicates. He "saved others" when, for example, he visited the home of Zacchaeus the tax collector and announced that "today salvation has come to this house. . . . For the Son of man came to seek and to save the lost."[19] The Son of man did not come to save himself, however. Others are saved while he is lost; they are saved, but at his expense. In that sense, he dies as their *substitute*. For all its limitations, this term pinpoints the unintended truth concealed within the rulers' taunts, a truth that encompasses the entire gospel narrative. To view Jesus' death as substitutionary need not imply that God himself is somehow obliged to punish sin while remaining free to inflict that punishment on someone other than the guilty party—in this case (because he is gracious) on his own Son. Rather, the concept of substitution draws attention to the contrast between the Son of

16. Mark 15:31b–32.
17. Matt. 27:42–43.
18. Luke 23:40–41.
19. Luke 19:9–10.

God's unreserved participation in the depths of human misery and the well-being he achieves for others. He dies so that they may live.[20]

Jesus' descent into the abyss is graphically portrayed in the gospel accounts. As all four evangelists note, he is deprived of his clothing and exposed to malicious public gaze in humiliating nakedness and helplessness. The mockery heaped on him by passers-by and rulers is evoked by his objective situation as a crucified person, contemptible as such. This is the reality expressed in a quotation from Isaiah 53:12 found in some manuscripts of Mark, which Eusebius includes in his analysis:

> And with him they crucified two thieves, one on his right, the other on his left, and the scripture was fulfilled that says, "And he was reckoned with the lawless."[21]

Although the Isaiah quotation is absent from most manuscripts, it is particularly apt here—more so perhaps than in the Luke context from which it has been transplanted. At the close of Luke's Last Supper narrative, Jesus mysteriously informs his disciples that earlier instructions about traveling light are canceled and that new requirements are in force:

> "Let one who has not sell his cloak and buy a sword. For I tell you, what is written must be fulfilled in me: 'And he was reckoned with the lawless.' For what is written about me has its fulfillment." And they said, "Lord, look, here are two swords!" And he said, "It is enough."[22]

Perhaps the appeal to Scripture is intended to explain why at least one disciple has a sword in the garden of Gethsemane, and uses it.[23] Surrounding oneself with an armed guard is the behavior of the "lawless," with whom Jesus must now be "reckoned" in accordance with the scriptural testimony. Entering the gospel tradition via Luke, the

20. See S. Gathercole, *Defending Substitution*.
21. Mark 15:28.
22. Luke 22:36b–38.
23. Matt. 26:51–52; Mark 14:47; Luke 22:49–51; John 18:10–11.

Isaiah passage was later transferred to Mark by someone who felt it
to be more appropriate to Jesus' crucifixion between two criminals.
In its original context in Isaiah, the passage emphasizes the contradiction between what appears to be the case—that the suffering servant
of the Lord belongs to the category of the "lawless"—and the reality
that he "bears the sins of many."[24]

Jesus' physical pain is not emphasized, though the reader can only
assume that it must have been extreme. There is just one possible
reference to physical suffering in the gospels, when the Fourth Evangelist has Jesus say, "I thirst," thus providing a context for the strange
offer of the vinegar-filled sponge, reported without explanation in
Matthew and Mark and seen by Luke as another form of mockery.[25]
For John, receiving the vinegar is somehow a necessary precondition
for Jesus' death, which occurs immediately afterward. Physical suffering does not seem to be the issue here. Far more significant than
the physical and psychological torment that Jesus experiences along
with other victims of crucifixion is the darkness that occasions his
cry of Godforsakenness:

> And from the sixth hour darkness came upon the whole land until
> the ninth hour. And at about the ninth hour Jesus cried out with a
> loud voice, saying, "Eli, eli, lema sabachthani," that is, "My God,
> my God, why have you forsaken me?" Some of those who stood there
> and heard were saying, "This man is calling upon Elijah." . . . Others
> said, "Wait, let us see if Elijah comes to save him." And Jesus cried
> out again with a loud voice and yielded up his spirit.[26]

The references to the sixth and the ninth hours are related to
a chronological note found in Mark alone: "It was the third hour
when they crucified him."[27] Jesus is crucified at the third hour and
dies at the ninth, and the darkness at the sixth hour divides the time

24. Isa. 53:12 LXX.
25. John 19:28–29; cf. Matt. 27:48; Mark 15:36; Luke 23:36.
26. Matt. 27:45–50; cf. Mark 15:33–37.
27. Mark 15:25.

of his suffering on the cross into two equal periods of three hours each. The first three-hour period is characterized by the parting of the garments and the mockery. To this ill-treatment Jesus does not respond; he simply endures it. In the second period the mocking voices fall silent as darkness descends at noon. Three hours later the silence is broken by the cry of Godforsakenness, in which the meaning of the darkness is disclosed to the reader, though not to the uncomprehending bystanders. Together, the darkness and the cry reveal the truth of the contemptuous claim that, though he saved others, he could not save himself. Jesus' ability to save others is dependent on his inability to save himself from physical and spiritual destruction.

Pattern

As he is crucified, the Lukan Jesus prays, "Father, forgive them, for they do not know what they are doing."[28] Although the passage is missing from some early manuscripts and may be a later insertion, it was present in Eusebius's text and is identified in his analysis as a passage unique to Luke.[29] In most of the manuscripts that include it, it is introduced with the words "And Jesus was saying" rather than the more usual "And Jesus said." The point may be that he continued to pray this prayer as he was being crucified, more concerned for his tormenters than for himself. In this extreme situation his actions embody his own earlier teaching:

> But I say to you who hear: love your enemies, do good to those who hate you, bless those who curse you, pray for those who abuse you.[30]

Love for the enemy is the ultimate form of the love of neighbor that Jesus illustrates in his parable of the good Samaritan, in response to

28. Luke 23:34.
29. See R. Swanson, *New Testament Greek Manuscripts: Luke*, 396; B. Metzger, *Textual Commentary*, 180.
30. Luke 6:27–28.

the question "Who is my neighbor?"[31] For Jesus, the neighbor is not simply the person who is like oneself: "If you love those who love you, what credit is that to you? Even sinners love those who love them."[32] The neighbor is the person whom one encounters in his or her need, irrespective of likeness or unlikeness; love of neighbor is a response to that need. At Golgotha, the sinister "Place of the Skull,"[33] Jesus' neighbors are those who carry out the work of crucifixion, who are as intimately present to him as the Samaritan is to the man who fell among thieves, but who intend his harm rather than his good. Yet at that moment of proximity they are his neighbors. Jesus does not cast himself in the role of the wounded man who, if he had been conscious, might have pleaded for help as the priest and the Levite hurried past him on their way from Jerusalem to Jericho. He does not seek a neighbor to minister to his own need, extreme though that is. Although he has every reason to identify himself with the victim in his own story, he identifies himself instead with the neighbor who acts to meet another's need, even when that other is the enemy who is depriving him of life itself. It makes no difference that this enemy is utterly unaware of any such need. Acts of violence and injustice defy the order of the one whom Jesus addresses as "Father," and those who perpetrate them need to be reconciled to that order whether they are aware of it or not.

Not all Jesus' neighbors at Golgotha are his enemies. He is able to act as neighbor to one who unexpectedly turns to him in his need, assuring him, "Today you will be with me in Paradise."[34] Jesus has himself fallen among thieves, and in his presence one of them becomes suddenly aware that the violent conduct that led to his own crucifixion was unjustified and indefensible. Just as the good Samaritan conducted the wounded man to an inn where he could be cared for and healed, so Jesus will escort his companion in suffering to the place of healing that he calls "Paradise." Turning from Luke to John, we find that Jesus'

31. Luke 10:29.
32. Luke 6:32.
33. Matt. 27:33; Mark 15:22; Luke 23:33; John 19:17.
34. Luke 23:43.

mother and the anonymous "disciple whom he loved" are also among his neighbors at Golgotha. As her firstborn son, it is Jesus' responsibility to make provision for Mary, and he entrusts her not to his "brothers," mentioned collectively and unfavorably earlier in this gospel, but to a disciple who will perhaps prove to be a surrogate for Jesus himself.[35]

In all three synoptic gospels, love of the neighbor is closely associated with the love of God. Luke's "lawyer" who questions Jesus about the definition of "neighbor" is commended for tracing the entire law back to the double requirement that "you shall love the Lord your God with all your heart and with all your soul and with all your strength and with all your mind, and your neighbor as yourself."[36] At Golgotha, love of neighbor is subject to extreme pressure; but so too is love of God. Yet Luke's Jesus ends his ordeal as he began it, by addressing God as Father: "Father, into your hands I commit my spirit."[37]

Life

The moment of Jesus' death is necessarily recorded in all four gospels, and it falls under Eusebius's canon I. In John, it is followed by a substantial postscript that tells how the dead Jesus' bones were left unbroken, although his side was pierced by a spear thrust.[38] There is nothing in the synoptic gospels that corresponds to this. Each event— the preservation of Jesus' bones and the perforation of his side—is said to fulfill scriptural prophecy. It is written of the Passover lamb that "not a bone of it shall be broken."[39] According to the Fourth Evangelist, Jesus' death coincides with the slaughter of the Passover lambs, although this point remains undeveloped.[40] It is also written that "they shall look upon the one whom they pierced."[41] Yet there

35. John 19:25–27; cf. 2:12; 7:3–5.
36. Luke 10:26–28.
37. Luke 23:46.
38. John 19:31–37.
39. John 19:36; cf. Exod. 12:46.
40. John 18:28, 39; cf. 13:1.
41. John 19:37; cf. Zech. 12:10.

is more to that spear thrust than a fulfillment of prophecy, which is perhaps cited for apologetic reasons, to demonstrate that Jesus' death has been scripted in advance, down to the last detail. From Jesus' perforated side there flow blood and water, and that detail is traced back not to Scripture but to an eyewitness testimony:

> One of the soldiers pierced his side with a spear, and immediately blood and water came forth. And the one who saw it has testified to it, and his testimony is true, and he knows that he speaks truth, so that you may believe.[42]

It is all very mysterious. Why does the outpoured blood and water require its own special testimony as a unique aid to faith? Who is the anonymous witness? He cannot easily be identified with the equally anonymous "disciple whom Jesus loved," for that disciple had already left the scene to escort Jesus' mother to his own home.[43] Whoever the witness may be, why is the truth of his testimony so emphatically asserted, as though in the face of skeptical objections? It seems that faith itself stands or falls with the truth of the witness's claim. The blood and water that he claims to have seen must be more than just blood and water. They must be life giving, a river flowing from its source in Jesus' pierced side.

The unbroken body of the Passover Lamb of God, the outflow of blood and water—the key to these mysteries is to be found earlier in the Gospel of John.

In John 6, the traditional story of the feeding of the five thousand is followed by a uniquely Johannine dialogue between Jesus and the crowd that takes place not at the site of the miracle but in the synagogue at Capernaum on the following day.[44] In the dialogue, the significance of the miracle is disputed. As so often in this gospel, Jesus and his audience are at cross-purposes. They demand that he provide them with a perpetual supply of bread, as Moses did with

42. John 19:34–35.
43. John 19:27.
44. John 6:59.

the manna in the wilderness.[45] Jesus urges them "not to labor for the food that perishes but for the food that endures to eternal life, which the Son of man will give you."[46] As the dialogue develops and as the audience's incomprehension deepens into hostility, Jesus identifies himself with the food that endures to eternal life, the typological equivalent of the scriptural manna from heaven: "I am the bread that came down from heaven."[47] Later still, in a further paradoxical turn, the bread turns into meat—"The bread that I shall give for the life of the world is my flesh"—which provokes the outraged question "How can this man give us his flesh to eat?"[48] The answer simply repeats and exacerbates the offense of the claim:

> Jesus said to them, "Truly, truly, I say to you, unless you eat the flesh of the Son of man and drink his blood, you have no life in you. Those who eat my flesh and drink my blood have eternal life, and I will raise them up at the Last Day."[49]

Against this background, the unbroken bones of the Passover Lamb of God and the blood flowing from his pierced side begin to make sense—although that sense remains utterly strange and counterintuitive. Jesus corresponds both to the manna from heaven and to the Passover lamb; he may be consumed in both roles. The anonymous witness's testimony to the blood and water sees in the physical blood the sign or sacrament of the life-giving drink bestowed on those who believe.

That drink is blood, but it is also water. After being abandoned by many of his followers in Galilee, Jesus travels to Jerusalem in John 7 for the Feast of Tabernacles. On the last day of the feast, we are told that he stood and proclaimed:

> "Any who thirst, let them come to me, and let those who believe in me drink." (As the scripture says, "Rivers of living water will flow from

45. John 6:30–34.
46. John 6:27.
47. John 6:41; cf. 6:34–35.
48. John 6:51–52.
49. John 6:53–54.

his heart.") This he said about the Spirit, which those who believed in him were to receive; for the Spirit was not yet present, as Jesus had not yet been glorified.[50]

It is the spear thrust following the death of Jesus that causes the rivers of living water to flow from his heart. Here, in another kaleidoscopic shift in the scriptural imagery, the background is to be found in Ezekiel's vision of a restored temple from whose threshold life-giving water pours forth; Jesus is identified with the temple just as he is with the manna and the Passover lamb.[51] He himself was thirsty as his death approached, yet life-giving rivers flowed from his side so that no one else would ever need to thirst.

Aftermath

There are minor anomalies in Eusebius's analysis of the burial and empty-tomb narratives, in particular the distinction he makes between the named women of Matthew and Mark and the unnamed women of Luke. More significantly, the analysis draws attention to the pivotal role of Mark throughout this sequence. Although Matthew, Luke, and John each makes his own unique contribution (the $X_{1,3,4}$ passages), Mark is always the common factor elsewhere. Other canons represented here all include Mark (I, II, VI, VIII; see table 7.2).

Eusebius's analysis of the gospel Easter stories is based on the oldest surviving version of Mark's gospel, which concluded at 16:8. At Jesus' empty tomb, Mary Magdalene and the other women encounter an angelic figure who announces his resurrection and instructs them to pass on to the male disciples a message about a reunion in Galilee. Remarkably enough, the women utterly fail to carry out this commission. The gospel ends by reporting that failure: "And going out they fled from the tomb, for terror and amazement had come

50. John 7:37–39.
51. Cf. Ezek. 47:1–12.

Table 7.2

Eusebian Canon/ Theme		Matthew	Mark	Luke	John
VI	Named women disciples	347 / 27:55–56	226 / 15:40–41		
I	Joseph's request	348 / 27:57–58	227 / 15:42–45	332 / 23:50–52	206 / 19:38
X₄	Nicodemus provides spices				207 / 19:39
I	The burial	349 / 27:59–60	228 / 15:46	333 / 23:53	208 / 19:40–42
VI	Witness of the burial	350 / 27:61	229 / 15:47		
X₁	The guard	351 / 27:62–66			
X₃	Imminent Sabbath; women			334 / 23:54–55	
VIII	The spices		230 / 16:1	335 / 23:56	
I	The stone rolled away	352 / 28:1–4	231 / 16:2–5	336 / 24:1–4	209 / 20:1
X₄	The race to the tomb				210 / 20:2–10
I	The angelic encounter	353 / 28:5–7	232 / 16:6–7	337 / 24:5–8	211 / 20:11–12
II	The departure from the tomb	354 / 28:8	233 / 16:8	338 / 24:9	

upon them, and they said nothing to anyone; for they were afraid."[52] Although Eusebius assigns this passage to his canon II, its Markan form is quite different from its Matthean and Lukan parallels. In Matthew the women run from the tomb "in fear *and great joy, to tell his disciples*"; immediately they meet the risen Lord himself.[53] Luke reports the actual communication of the message—and that it was disbelieved.[54] Matthew, Luke, and John all proceed to recount

52. Mark 16:8.
53. Matt. 28:8–9.
54. Luke 24:9–11.

appearances of the risen Lord. For Mark, however, the empty-tomb story is an ending rather than a new beginning.

The question is whether a gospel *should* end where Mark originally ended. For the other evangelists, it is essential for the risen Jesus to reveal himself to his disciples in his risen body and commission them for their future role as proclaimers of the gospel. The disciples must be brought to faith in the risen Lord, and they must then communicate that faith to others, gentiles as well as Jews. At some point in the second century, Mark's apparent indifference to these concerns came to seem intolerable. A new ending was composed and tacked on to the old one:

> And going out they fled from the tomb, for terror and amazement had come upon them, and they said nothing to anyone; for they were afraid. And when he rose early on the first day of the week, he appeared first to Mary Magdalene, from whom he had cast out seven demons. She went and told those who had been with him as they grieved and wept. When they heard that he was alive and had been seen by her, they did not believe it.[55]

This so-called Longer Ending of Mark proceeds to describe an appearance to two disciples as they walk into the country and a meeting with all eleven remaining disciples in which they are criticized for their unbelief and then equipped for worldwide mission.[56]

In spite of the Longer Ending, texts concluding at Mark 16:8 continued to circulate. Several centuries later, a new attempt was made to provide a more satisfactory conclusion to this gospel. This is the so-called Shorter Ending, not to be confused with the earlier ending at 16:8, which is shorter still:

> And going out they fled from the tomb, for terror and amazement had come upon them, and they said nothing to anyone; for they were afraid. And they reported briefly to Peter and those with him all that they had

55. Mark 16:8–11.
56. Mark 16:12–20.

been told. Afterward Jesus himself sent out through them, from east to
west, the holy and imperishable message of eternal salvation. Amen.

Here it is assumed that the women were fearful and silent only until
they reached the male disciples, who presumably believed their message. As in the Longer Ending, together with Matthew, Luke, and
John, the risen Lord's appearance to his disciples is associated especially with the call to mission. Notably absent from all these texts
is the link between Jesus' resurrection and the general resurrection
of the dead, so strongly emphasized by Paul and later writers.[57] As
in the case of Jesus' death, his resurrection might be interpreted in
a variety of ways. One such interpretation may be recovered if the
Longer and Shorter Endings of Mark are set aside and the original
ending is restored.

If Mark originally concluded with the women's terrified departure
from the tomb, the angelic proclamation of Jesus' resurrection is this
evangelist's only direct testimony to this event:

> Do not be amazed! You seek Jesus the Nazarene, who was crucified.
> He has been raised, he is not here, see the place where they laid him.[58]

In the other gospels, where the empty-tomb story is the start of a sequence of Easter narratives, it is the Lord's appearances that evoke faith
in his resurrection rather than the angelic proclamation. Indeed, if the
angelic message communicated through the women is disbelieved, as
it is in Luke and the Longer Ending, the empty-tomb story is deprived
of real significance. But if Mark's testimony to Jesus' resurrection is
wholly contained within this story, then its role is greatly enhanced.
The question is how that enhanced role is to be understood.

In its original Markan form the empty-tomb story looks backward
to Jesus' death and burial rather than forward to his appearances.
Mary Magdalene, Mary the mother of James and Joses, and Salome
are introduced as "looking on from afar" as the dead Jesus hangs on

57. Cf. 1 Cor. 15.
58. Mark 16:6.

the cross.[59] It is the same three women who bring spices to the tomb on Easter morning, and two of them are also said to have witnessed his burial.[60] Other figures play a more restricted role in the closing stages of Mark's story. Joseph of Arimathea asks permission to bury Jesus; Pilate grants his request after consultation with the centurion; the young man in white delivers his message at the tomb. Although silent except when discussing the problem of the stone, the women are present at all three critical moments: the death of Jesus, his burial, his empty tomb. The effect is to turn the empty-tomb story into a direct sequel to the burial. The unseen divine action that leaves the tomb empty of Jesus' body reverses Joseph's action in placing it there. The women are witnesses both of the laying out of the body in the tomb and of its disappearance: "See the place where they laid him!" The disappearance of the body must be explained, and that explanation is the sole extent of Mark's testimony to the resurrection: "He is not here, he is risen!"[61]

Death, burial, resurrection: the question is how the three events are to be coordinated. The weight of the narrative lies overwhelmingly on the first of these. Already in Mark's passion predictions the resurrection on the third day seems little more than a postscript to a catalogue of future sufferings that culminate in death.[62] The burial and the resurrection may be seen as contrasting human and divine responses to that death. Joseph's courageous and generous action seeks to restore a measure of dignity to Jesus' mistreated body. The powerful and unseen divine action occurs on a quite different plane. It declares and confirms that in his death the Son of man fulfilled his vocation, which was "to give his life as a ransom for many,"[63] securing their well-being by submitting himself to physical and spiritual annihilation.

59. Mark 15:40–41.
60. Mark 16:1; 15:47.
61. Mark 16:6.
62. Mark 10:33–34; cf. 8:31; 9:31.
63. Mark 10:45.

8

The Truth of the Gospel

Around half a century before the birth of Christ, the Roman poet Titus Lucretius Carus composed a philosophical poem in six books ambitiously entitled *De rerum natura*. A literal translation of the title does not quite capture the scope of the poet's ambition. Rather than *On the Nature of Things*, a translator might select *On the Nature of the Universe*. Better still would be *A Theory of Everything*. Lucretius's poem is of its time, but its main arguments can be transferred all too easily into a contemporary context. The poem teaches that everything in the universe is made up of an infinite number of material particles, "atoms" drifting eternally through an equally infinite space. These atoms have an inbuilt tendency to unite and so to form the complex entities of the world we inhabit: stars and winds, rocks and trees, bodies and minds. Things come into being, persist for a while, and then dissolve as the atoms that compose them form new configurations. The atoms are just there. They always have been, and they always will be. No god has created them. We cannot go round the back of them to discover hidden divine agencies directing the forces of nature, for no such agencies exist. Indeed, the poem wants to free us from our dependence on these imaginary agencies. It teaches that we would be much happier without them.

Near the beginning of his poem Lucretius addresses himself to a reader unsettled by his demand that familiar religious beliefs and practices should simply be abandoned. To demonstrate his thesis that religion is a source of great evils, he retells an old story about a father who sacrifices an innocent child in order to obtain the favor of the gods.[1] In this case the child is a girl, Iphigenia, summoned to Aulis by her father, Agamemnon, in order to celebrate her marriage. As she arrives for the ceremony, she notices that the crowds are weeping. So too is her own father, who stands behind the altar next to the priests, who are bearing knives. There is no sacrificial animal in sight, and there will be no wedding: her father has deceived her. He has made ready to sail for Troy, but he has offended the goddess Diana and his ships are becalmed. If he is to obtain a favorable wind from the goddess, he must sacrifice his own daughter. Suddenly grasping the truth of her situation, Iphigenia falls in terror to the ground and has to be dragged to the altar, where the necessary deed is done. The innocent atones for the guilty, and the fleet can sail off into the sunset. The moral of the story is summed up in a single devastating line: *Tantum religio potuit suadere malorum*—this is the extent to which religion can persuade people to commit the most atrocious actions.[2] Even loving parents—Agamemnon, Abraham—are not immune from its persuasive power. The poet's conviction of the evils of religion would in no way be diminished if it were to be said even of a deity that he "did not spare his only Son but gave him up for us all."[3]

Although it will not have escaped Lucretius's notice that religion takes many forms, he is struck more by similarities than by differences. Always and everywhere, religion has created rites and techniques for negotiating human relationships with unseen powers behind the visible phenomena of the world, powers that control and direct those

---

1. Lucretius, *On the Nature of Things* 1.82–101.
2. Lucretius, *On the Nature of Things* 1.101.
3. Rom. 8:32.

phenomena so as to bring blessing to those they favor and the opposite to those they do not. Religion's rites and techniques are normally the preserve of a class of professionals whose proximity to the divine equips them for an advocacy role on behalf of their human clients. For Lucretius, this is all falsehood and mystification. If the winds are in the wrong direction, that has nothing to do with the wrath of the gods. If the winds are in the right direction, it is not because divine wrath has been appeased by costly sacrifices. Winds are just winds, not expressions of some superhuman benevolence or displeasure. They blow where they will, observing a logic intrinsic to the world's material substructure.

In presenting his readers with his theory of everything, Lucretius invites them to join a community. His community has a founder who, though human, has far more right to be regarded as divine than any traditional god—such are the benefits he has brought to the human race. Throughout his poem the poet eloquently expounds the philosophy of Epicurus, who, two centuries before Lucretius's birth, taught his philosophy to a group of men and women who met together in the garden of his house in Athens. In contrast, the community to which the poet invites his readers is dispersed. It exists wherever the poem achieves its persuasive aim, which is to draw others into its world—the real world as imagined in the poem, in which there are only atoms and the space that contains them but no deities. Like all other communities of the like-minded, this one has its dogmas, and subscribing to them is a condition of membership. One such dogma is that religion is inherently evil and that human beings fully realize their humanity only when they reject religion. Differentiation, nuance, and counterexample are not welcome here, and self-critique is permitted only so long as it does not threaten the fundamentals. Another dogmatic commitment is to the possibility and plausibility of a singular "theory of everything" that accounts seamlessly and comprehensively for all that is. Lucretius's poem circles around these two communal commitments, one positive and the other negative.

From a "humanist" perspective of this kind, any text that speaks of a human relationship to a divine world rests on a dangerously distorted account of the nature of things (*rerum natura*). Self-evidently, this applies also to the New Testament and its four gospels. From this humanist or secularist standpoint, the gospels weave a tapestry of pure fictions around a bare minimum of historical fact but are nevertheless supposed to embody truth in its most absolute and totalitarian form. Blind faith in that truth is demanded, and the person of another faith or no faith is demonized. The gospels' claim that divine authority is uniquely present in a single individual opens them to all kinds of ideological abuse by the powerful at the expense of the weak. The fact that the key roles are played by a Father, a Son, and twelve specially selected males continues to disenfranchise women in ways that are now unacceptable and incomprehensible in the enlightened secular world. Equally problematic is the gospels' representation of a parent/child relationship in which the suffering of the son is deemed good, right, and necessary by the father. Texts that bestow transcendent validity on the marginalization of women or the abuse of children are in no way sacrosanct or beyond criticism. Where they are held to be such, however, there is no authentic freedom to challenge their right to this status. The still-potent charge of "blasphemy" lies ready to hand if contradictions, absurdities, and immoralities are pointed out.

And so on. There is a time and place for responding to these issues, but it is not here. Yet even if one rejects the secularist consensus that the gospel is false and detrimental to human well-being, its allegation of gospel falsehood may still provoke reflection on the question of gospel truth. As with most truths and truth claims, the first step must be to identify their primary contexts. Some truths are no doubt universal and universally acknowledged. The question of their truth or falsehood does not arise, and there is no room for debate. Other, perhaps more interesting truths or truth claims are embedded in communities and must be observed *in situ*. They do not exist in the abstract, and there are no universally applicable criteria for assessing them. That may be the case when the truth in question is the truth of the gospel. In the following four case studies we will uncover ways in which gospel truth has been asserted in the past, in the hope that these will prove instructive for the present.

The Eucharistic Milieu

In an engaging piece of autobiography, the second-century Christian philosopher Justin Martyr tells how he passed from one teacher of philosophy to another without attaining the truth and certainty he sought. One, a Stoic, understood the pursuit of philosophy as something other than the quest for God. Another, a Peripatetic, proved too expensive. Turned down by a distinguished Pythagorean because of his ignorance of music, astronomy, and geometry, the young Justin seemed to find what he was looking for when he joined a Platonist school and learned to love the higher immaterial realms in which, as it seemed, God was to be found. Seeking solitude for contemplation by the sea, Justin finds himself followed by an elderly man who engages him in philosophical conversation and begins to undermine his newfound Platonic faith in the knowability of God and the immortality of the soul. After reducing Justin to despair, the old man recommends that he abandon his enthusiasm for the Greek philosophers and turn instead to the Hebrew prophets, men of still-greater antiquity who announced in advance the coming into the world of the Son of God. At that promising juncture the old man abruptly departs. "Immediately," Justin tells us, "a fire was lit within my soul, and love for the prophets and those who are friends of Christ took hold of me, and, as I reflected on his words, I found this alone to be the certain and profitable philosophy."[4] Justin is in his own eyes still a philosopher, yet he now loves and associates with all who are "friends of Christ," whether philosophers or not. He has exchanged a community of Platonists for the Christian community, and in so doing

4. Justin Martyr, *Dialogue with Trypho* 8.1.

he has moved from one world to another. The world as experienced from within the Christian community will be a very different place from the various philosophical worlds in which he had tried unsuccessfully to make his home.

At the heart of this new communal life are the texts that Justin calls "the memoirs of the apostles," although, as he admits, everyone else calls them "gospels." These texts are for all people alike, irrespective of their social background or educational level:

> On the day called "Sunday" there is a meeting of all who live in the towns and the countryside, and the memoirs of the apostles or the writings of the prophets are read for as long as time permits. Then when the reader has finished, the president makes an address that instructs and encourages us to imitate these good things. Then we all stand and pray, and . . . when our prayer is ended, bread, wine, and water are brought.[5]

This is the communal context that nurtures Justin's conviction that the apostolic and prophetic Scriptures speak truth. Their truth does not come fully to light as they are merely read, however. These voices from the sacred past must be complemented by the speech of a contemporary, the preacher whose homily makes the connection between the readings and the weekday lives of his hearers from town or countryside. Without such a connection, renewed every Sunday, the gospels would be "true" only in a limited sense. They might speak truthfully about people who really lived and events that really happened, but they would hardly provide the encompassing, livable truth that they intend. The truth of the gospel is not some inert correspondence between text and referent. Its capacity to transform must constantly be rediscovered as the gospels are read, interpreted, heard, prayed, and lived. The president's verbal interpretation of the gospel reading aims to show how a more comprehensive gospel interpretation can be practiced in daily life.

5. Justin Martyr, *1 Apology* 67.3–5.

This connection between gospel and life is not an arbitrary one. In Justin's brief but revealing description of early Christian worship, the gospel narratives are not only read and interpreted but also reenacted in the celebration of the Eucharist. After the reading, the homily, and the prayers, bread and wine are brought because Jesus instructed his followers to remember him in that way:

> For the apostles, in their memoirs which are called "gospels," handed down to us what they were commanded, that Jesus taking bread and giving thanks said, "Do this in remembrance of me, this is my body," and that taking the cup likewise and giving thanks he said, "This is my blood." And to them alone he imparted it.[6]

In the Eucharist participants find themselves located within the gospel narrative as disciples of Jesus who share a meal at which he offers them himself as their food and drink. This reenactment of the Last Supper is the objective basis for the "imitation" (*mimesis*) that occurs in daily life, informed by the gospel reading and the homily. Justin elsewhere shows himself to be more familiar with Matthew and Luke than with Mark and John, and that is the case here too. The command to "do this in remembrance of me" is taken from Luke, who here follows Paul.[7] For Justin, as for Luke, this command is crucially important as the only explicit indication that Jesus' actions are to be repeated by his followers. In Justin the command to reenact is given still greater emphasis than in Luke by being placed before the words about the bread and the cup. Also Lukan is the first reference to "giving thanks," where Matthew speaks instead of "pronouncing a blessing."[8] Justin follows Luke in highlighting the symmetry between Jesus' actions in the term "likewise." By adding the definite article in the reference to "the cup," both writers indicate that this cup is familiar to readers from their own participation in the Eucharist. In Lukan sequence these passages are as follows:

6. Justin Martyr, *1 Apology* 66.3.
7. Luke 22:19; cf. 1 Cor. 11:24–25.
8. Matt. 26:26.

> And taking bread and *giving thanks* he broke it and gave it to
>   them . . .
> "*Do this in remembrance of me* . . ."
> And *the cup likewise after supper* . . .⁹

On the other hand, the simplified words of institution ("This is
my body," "This is my blood"), along with "taking a cup and giving
thanks" and the reference to the disciples' participation in it, echo
Matthew:

> "Take, *eat, this is my body*."
> And *taking a cup and giving thanks* he gave it to them . . .
> "*This is my blood* of the new covenant poured out for many
>   for the forgiveness of sins."¹⁰

In Justin's summary the Matthean and Lukan eucharistic narratives are woven together. There is also a Johannine dimension to
Justin's eucharistic language. Jesus' gifts of self at the Last Supper
are a symbolic representation of his incarnate life as a whole. The
synoptic eucharistic language is placed in a broad Johannine context:

> As through the word of God Jesus Christ our Savior was made flesh
> [*sarkopoiētheis*] and had flesh and blood for our salvation, so (as
> we have been taught) the nourishment for which thanks are offered
> through the prayer of his word . . . is the flesh and blood of the Jesus
> who was made flesh.¹¹

Johannine influence is perceptible here in the double reference to Jesus
being "made flesh" and in the association of his "flesh and blood"
with the Eucharist, in contrast to the synoptic "body and blood."¹²
The incorporation of this Johannine perspective ensures that what
is recollected in the Eucharist is not the death of Jesus considered
in isolation but his self-giving death as the goal and meaning of his

9. Luke 22:19–20.
10. Matt. 26:26–28; cf. Mark 14:22–24.
11. Justin Martyr, *1 Apology* 66.2.
12. John 1:14; 6:54.

entire incarnate life. It is, as it were, the whole Jesus who is imparted in the bread and wine, the Jesus of the full gospel narrative extending from incarnation to crucifixion and beyond. And it is the entire self-giving act of this Jesus as narrated in the canonical gospel that is reenacted in every Eucharist.

Justin's description of an early Christian Eucharist is, in one sense, uninformative. Everything is as we would expect. Christians gather together for Sunday worship, there are readings from the gospels or the Old Testament and a homily based on them, followed by general intercessions, the eucharistic prayer, and the distribution of the bread and the wine; a collection is also taken for those in need. While it is not clear whether the words of institution are incorporated into the eucharistic prayer, the fact that Justin cites them means that they are well understood as the basis for eucharistic worship. Everything is as we would expect because everything here remains familiar. Reenactment of Jesus' last supper still continues along very similar lines, every Sunday. This literal reenactment may still be seen as the basis for a *mimesis* articulated in gospel reading and homily and practiced in daily life, without any sense of strain or artificiality. Within this eucharistic context, it is natural to affirm and unnatural to deny the truth of the gospel in its fourfold canonical form.

Evangelical Apologetics

When Jesus was accused by false witnesses at his trial, he remained silent. He might have spoken up in his own defense, but he chose not to do so. Even now (so Origen remarks as he opens his great apologetic treatise *Against Celsus*) Jesus maintains his silence when he and his followers are attacked by hostile critics, as they always will be so long as evil persists in the world. His only defense—and it is a risky one—is the life of the community he founded. Christians would do well to follow their Lord's example and keep silence when they come across anti-Christian tracts like the one Origen has to hand. The tract in question is the *True Discourse*, written many years earlier by Celsus but still in circulation in the 240s as Origen responds to it. Origen concedes that an apologia for Christian faith might actually weaken it by diverting attention from the life of the community; silence may well be the better option. Yet he chooses instead to write, at the request of his faithful patron, Ambrosius, and out of consideration for the weaker fellow Christian whose faith might be shaken by Celsus's arguments.

Celsus knows that a number of versions of the gospel are in circulation, but he is familiar primarily with the Matthean one, which he seeks to subvert. According to Matthew, Jesus' mother conceived and bore him miraculously, while a virgin. Her intended husband, Joseph, initially suspected her of unfaithfulness but was persuaded by an angelic visitation that her child was indeed conceived by the power of the Holy Spirit. According to Celsus, that story is just pious fraud. What actually happened is that Mary committed adultery with a soldier named Panthera and was rejected by her carpenter husband.[13] Expelled from her home village, she wandered aimlessly for a while before arriving in Egypt with her illegitimate son; it was in Egypt that the child acquired the magical powers that convinced him that he was none other than the Son of God.[14] The evangelist conceals this unedifying reality behind a tissue of blatant falsehoods: prophecies fulfilled, magical stars, murderous monarchs, and the rest of it.

Then there is the story of Jesus' baptism. In his assault on the Matthean narrative, Celsus uses the device of a fictional Jewish interrogator who addresses Jesus directly. "When you were washing beside John," says Celsus's Jew with heavy irony, "you say that something having the appearance of a bird from the air alighted upon you. What credible witness saw this appearance, and who heard the voice from heaven adopting you as Son of God?"[15] For Celsus such gospel narratives are worthless fabrications that systematically distort the

---

13. Origen, *Against Celsus* 1.32.
14. Origen, *Against Celsus* 1.28.
15. Origen, *Against Celsus* 1.41.

unpalatable historical truth in order to promote and propagate the Christian ideology.

How can Christians accept as true a story that features heavens torn open, a descending dove, and a voice from on high? Behind the hostility Origen perceives a genuine question requiring a nuanced answer. It should be noted, he says, that reconstructing historical events and demonstrating that they actually occurred is always a difficult and delicate operation. In the end, much may have to be taken on trust—the historicity of the Trojan War, for example.[16] In critically assessing a work of history, we have three basic options. First, we may straightforwardly assent to its claims. Second, we may conclude that a nonliteral, figurative meaning is intended. Third, we may suspect that a story has been invented to serve the interests of particular persons or groups. Critical Christian readers must be aware especially of the second option as they engage with the history of Jesus as related in the gospels. Christians are not required to abandon their critical faculties and believe everything they read in exactly the same way.[17]

In the case of Jesus' baptism, Origen notes that the historicity of the two human protagonists—John and Jesus—is confirmed by a reputable source that cannot be accused of any pro-Christian bias. In book 18 of his *Antiquities of the Jews*, the Jewish historian Josephus speaks of John and his practice of the rite of baptism. Elsewhere he also speaks incidentally of Jesus himself, in a reference to the death of "James the Just, who was a brother of Jesus called Christ."[18] So Jesus' baptism by John is not itself implausible. There is no reason why we should not assent to the gospels' claim that this event truly occurred.

What of the opened heavens? Here Origen's second option comes into play: the gospels' language is figurative. We are not to suppose that the heavens were actually opened in the sense that the physical

16. Origen, *Against Celsus* 1.42.
17. Origen, *Against Celsus* 1.42.
18. Origen, *Against Celsus* 1.47, citing Josephus, *Antiquities* 18.116–19; 20.200.

structure of the universe was temporarily disrupted. This was not
the case when the prophet Ezekiel reported that "the heavens were
opened, and I saw visions of God,"[19] and the opening of the heavens at
Jesus' baptism would have been no different. The discerning Christian
reader must conclude that the prophetic and gospel texts are using
figurative language to describe visionary experiences.[20]

It is true, says Origen, that most Christian readers or hearers of
the gospels are not particularly discerning or critical, not having
had the educational advantages enjoyed by the few. As they hear
in the gospel reading that the heavens were opened, most ordinary
Christians will suppose that the physical structure of the universe
was momentarily altered. In the world they inhabit there is no difficulty in supposing that such things have happened, and to speak
to such people of figurative language would alarm them.[21] Celsus
is contemptuous of the naive and uneducated whose faith is blind
and who are incapable of critical reasoning.[22] Origen defends them.
Simple faith is entirely appropriate for uneducated people; if salvation
were open only to those with advanced critical faculties, those who
are saved would be few.[23] In addition, those who pride themselves
on their rationality should reflect on the role of faith in the choice
of a philosophical school, which is rarely based on a dispassionate
assessment of all available options.[24]

A critical reader may assent to either literal or figurative meaning
but may also *dissent* where a narrative seems shaped by extraneous
interests rather than concern for the truth. This is Origen's third
option, and it is essentially the reading strategy adopted by Celsus
himself. As a further example of the ideologically motivated falsity of
the gospel story, Celsus cites the claim that Jesus foresaw his death and
the events leading up to it—a claim he believes to have been fabricated

19. Ezek. 1:1.
20. Origen, *Against Celsus* 1.48.
21. Origen, *Against Celsus* 1.48.
22. Origen, *Against Celsus* 1.9.
23. Origen, *Against Celsus* 1.9.
24. Origen, *Against Celsus* 1.10.

by Jesus' disciples without any likely basis in reality.[25] On the evening of his arrest, Jesus is said to have predicted both that his disciples would abandon him and that Peter would deny him three times. Even if that were true (Celsus argues), it would make little difference; an evildoer who foresees his death is no less an evildoer. Most probably it is not true. Deeply embarrassed by Jesus' shameful and merited death, his disciples tried to mitigate the scandal by ascribing to him a supernatural knowledge of his own destiny.[26]

As Origen notes, there is just one problem with this reading. If Jesus' followers were so concerned to conceal embarrassing truths, why did they record the disciples' abandonment of Jesus and Peter's denials at all? The fact that events may have occurred does not force anyone to preserve a written record of them. As leaders of the Christian community, Peter and the other disciples had every reason to suppress their own abject failures on the night of Jesus' arrest. Yet they did not do so. Origen suggests that such narratives are a sign of the gospels' commitment to truth.[27]

The outcome of Origen's apologia for the gospel narrative is inconclusive. Given that Celsus is not committed in advance to the truth of the gospel, the legitimacy in principle of his "hermeneutic of suspicion" cannot be denied. Origen's evangelical apologetics cannot hope for the outright victory over an opponent that might be achieved in other spheres of conflict—the law court, the sporting arena, or the battlefield. Yet he can at least deny victory to his opponent and, more important, begin to develop a reading of the gospels that is both critical and Christian.

Form and Content

Toward the end of the preface to his German translation of the New Testament (1522), Martin Luther goes so far as to rank the books

25. Origen, *Against Celsus* 2.15.
26. Origen, *Against Celsus* 2.16.
27. Origen, *Against Celsus* 2.15.

of the New Testament in order of importance.[28] That such a ranking should be attempted at all is extraordinary, and it is hard to find
analogies before or since.

At the upper end of the scale stand the Gospel and First Epistle
of John alongside the Pauline Epistles, with Romans, Galatians, and
Ephesians singled out for special mention; 1 Peter is added to lend
further apostolic weight to this subcollection of books on which every
true Christian ought to meditate daily. At the lower end of the scale
stands the Epistle of James. Notoriously, Luther dubs it "an epistle
of straw" that "has nothing of the nature of the gospel about it" (*eyn
rechte stroern Epistel . . . , denn sie doch keyn Evangelisch art an ihr
hat*).[29] The Gospels of Matthew, Mark, and Luke are placed between
the two extremes. Ten books altogether are mentioned by name here,
six at the top end (along with the rest of the Pauline collection), one
at the bottom end, and three in the middle. The three main points
on this scale are distant from one another, separated by great tracts
of empty space. The Gospel of John is *far, far* preferable to the other
three gospels; it is placed *high* over them (*den andern dreyen weyt
weyt fur zu zihen vnd hoher zu heben*).[30] In the last resort one could
dispense with Matthew, Mark, and Luke, which focus on Christ's
works rather than his preaching—that is, his proclamation of salvation as reported by John.

Luther did not rearrange the order of the New Testament books to
reflect his rankings, except at one point. The Epistle to the Hebrews
is relegated to a position after the Petrine and Johannine Epistles.
The four texts that conclude the New Testament collection are now
Hebrews, James, Jude, and Revelation, which (Luther alleges) have
always been held in lower esteem than the undisputed canonical books.
The collection of seven Catholic Epistles is broken up, and a new
collection is formed that amounts to a New Testament equivalent of
the Old Testament Apocrypha. To underline this point, these final

28. *WA DB* 6.10–11; *LW* 35.361–62.
29. *WA DB* 6.10; *LW* 35.362.
30. *WA DB* 6.10; *LW* 35.362.

four books are not included in the enumeration Luther adds to the other books, from 1 to 23.

At the front end of the volume, Matthew, Mark, Luke, and John occur in the conventional order under conventional titles: *1. Euangelion Sanct Matthes*; *2. Euangelion Sanct Marcus*; *3. Euangelion Sanct Lucas*; *4. Euangelion Sanct Johanis*. Yet there is no longer any rationale either for the order or for the titles. The four-gospel collection has been broken up, at least in principle, along with the Catholic Epistles. Near the start of his preface Luther writes, "Therefore let it be known in the first place that the idea is to be rejected that there are four Gospels and only four Evangelists" (*Darumb ist auffs erste zu wissen, das abtzuthun ist der wahn, das vier Euangelia vnd nur vier Euangelisten sind*).[31] The traditional titles are misleading, for they apply the key term *Euangelion* to the literary genre of narratives about Christ, whereas the Greek loanword actually means "good message, good tidings, good news, a good report that one sings and tells with gladness" (*gute botschafft, gute meher, gutte newzeytung, gutt geschrey, dauon man singet, saget vnd frolich ist*).[32] The goodness and gladness of the gospel message are abundantly clear in the Gospel of John, in which Jesus speaks of himself as the bread of life, the light of the world, the good shepherd, and so on, addressing those who hunger, who walk in darkness, and who stray like lost sheep.[33] But Luther finds far less evidence of goodness or reason for gladness when he considers Matthew, Mark, and Luke. It seems that these so-called *euangelia* are unworthy of the name.

If taken seriously, such a conclusion would fundamentally undermine any attempt to rethink the fourfold gospel as a differentiated yet coherent whole. The canonical gospel would deviate from the truth of the gospel; the form of the New Testament as a whole would be subverted by a radical construal of its core content.[34] Yet in Luther's

31. *WA DB* 6.2; *LW* 35.357.
32. *WA DB* 6.2; *LW* 35.358.
33. Cf. John 6:35; 8:12; 10:14.
34. Such radicalism is, however, far more instructive than a bland biblicism that assigns an undifferentiated "authority" to every biblical text. That Luther's construal

New Testament the form persists. The twenty-seven books are all there in (almost) their familiar order; the radicalism is (largely) confined to Luther's prefaces. The question is whether "gospel" as literary genre and "gospel" as good and joyful news are really to be divided.

Remarkably, Luther offers a solution to the problem he created in a short text written in 1521 while he was at work on his New Testament translation. The text was composed to accompany a collection of sermons known as the Wartburg Postil and is entitled "A Brief Instruction on What One Should Seek and Expect in the Gospels" (*Eyn kleyn unterricht, was man ynn den Euangeliis suchen und gewartten soll*).[35] Unsurprisingly, many of the same points are made as in the preface to the New Testament, written shortly afterward. Here, however, there is no ranking of New Testament writings, nor is there a division of the fourfold gospel into a superior text, in which Christ proclaims the word of salvation, and inferior texts, which speak only of his works. The crucial distinction now lies not in the texts but in the reader. This point is already implicit in the title, in which "what one should seek and expect" refers to what the reader brings to the text as well as to what the text will say to the reader. More explicitly, there is a right approach to the text and a wrong approach. The right way to approach the text is to seek and expect to find in it Christ as the gift of God. The wrong way is to seek and expect to find Christ as an example to be imitated. While it is true that Christ is an example to be imitated, that must come second. Christ is first and foremost the gift of God. Only on that basis is he also the definitive pattern for our conduct:

> The chief article and foundation of the gospel is that, before you take Christ as an example, you first accept and recognize him as a gift and present that is given to you by God and is your own. So, when you see

---

of the New Testament continued to be fruitful into the twentieth century is illustrated by Rudolf Bultmann's *Theology of the New Testament*, in which the privileging of Paul and John over the synoptics is obviously derived from Luther. See F. Watson, "Bultmann and the Theological Interpretation of Scripture."

35. *WA* 10 I.8–18; *LW* 35.117–24.

or hear that he does or suffers something, you must not doubt that Christ himself with this doing or suffering is yours.

Das hauptstuck und grund des Euangelii ist, das du Christum zuvor, ehe du yhn zum exempel fassist, auffnehmist unnd erkennist als eyn gabe und geschenck, das dyr von gott geben und deyn eygen sey, also das, wenn du yhm zusihest odder horist, das er ettwas thutt odder leydet, das du nit zweyfellst, er selb Christus mit solchem thun und leyden sey deyn.[36]

In this single illuminating statement—just one sentence in German—an entire gospel hermeneutic is proposed. While Luther's emphasis on gift may reflect Pauline influence, the term is also deeply embedded in the gospels. In the Gospel of John it is said that "God so loved the world," or rather, "*Thus* God loved the world, that he *gave* his only Son, that everyone who believes in him should not perish but have eternal life."[37] (The *houtōs* with which this statement opens means "in this way" rather than "so much," making the divine love synonymous with the giving of the gift.) God's gift of the Son is also the Son's self-giving: "The bread that I shall *give* for the life of the world is my flesh."[38] Thus in the synoptic gospels Jesus breaks bread and *gives* it, saying (in the longer Lukan formulation), "This is my body *which is given for you*."[39] Similarly, the cup is *given*: the Greek verb occurs six times in the three synoptic accounts of the eucharistic self-giving. Elsewhere it is said that "the Son of man came not to be served but to serve and to *give* his life as a ransom for many."[40] These synoptic "gift" sayings are no less comprehensive than the Johannine ones, and they provide the textual basis for Luther's claim that what is to be sought and expected in the gospels is, first and foremost, Christ as gift. The difference between John and the synoptics here is more one of idiom than of substance.

36. *WA* 10 I.11; *LW* 35.119.
37. John 3:16.
38. John 6:51.
39. Luke 22:19; cf. Matt. 26:26; Mark 14:22.
40. Matt. 20:28; Mark 10:45.

Christ is *also* example, however. The gift opens the way to a new pattern of conduct modeled on Christ and possible only through the Christ-gift. First the gift, then the example:

> If I then, your Teacher and Lord, have washed your feet, you also ought to wash one another's feet. For I have given you an example, that you also should do as I have done to you.[41]

> As I have loved you, you also must love one another.[42]

In the synoptics too, Jesus is the exemplar of the conduct he requires. He tells his followers to love and pray for their enemies, and he himself loves and prays for his enemies as he is being crucified.[43] He pronounces beatitudes on the poor in spirit and the meek, and he himself is gentle and lowly in heart.[44] In all four gospels Christ is gift and example, and in that order. Christian conduct is always a response to gracious divine action. Otherwise, as Luther says, it is simply pagan.[45]

Since the gospels are at one here, there is no need to distance the form of the gospel from its content, the fourfold narrative from the message. In the end, Luther's instruction as to what to seek and expect is tautologous: in the gospel we are to seek and expect gospel, and we are to seek and expect it there because that is what it is.

The One Word

"The truth of the gospel"—the expression is from Paul, who uses it twice in the passage of polemical autobiography that opens the main body of his Letter to the Galatians.[46] Paul does not envisage a gospel text, let alone four of them. His concern is for the message of

41. John 13:14–15.
42. John 13:34.
43. Cf. Luke 6:27–28; 23:34.
44. Cf. Matt. 5:3, 5; 11:29.
45. *WA* 10 I.9; *LW* 35.117.
46. Gal. 2:5, 14.

the crucified and risen Jesus on which his Galatian communities are based, and specifically for the implications of its Jewish scriptural roots for gentile converts. Do those scriptural roots require gentile converts and communities to adopt recognizably Jewish practices, patterning their conduct on the law of Moses rather than on the gospel itself? In this context, maintaining "the truth of the gospel" means differentiating a practice grounded in the law from one grounded in the gospel.

In another context, "the truth of the gospel" might mean something quite different. In the marketplace of Athens, Paul debates the gospel with Epicurean and Stoic philosophers, and his topics there are Jesus and the resurrection rather than dietary laws and circumcision.[47] At Athens as in Galatia, the question of truth arises whenever the gospel is not simply preached or read but also challenged and debated. The challenge may arise from within the Christian community. In a moment of acute crisis, Paul can see the truth of the gospel as threatened not only by the anonymous individuals he describes as "false brothers" but even by leading names within the early Christian movement: Barnabas, his missionary colleague, and Cephas, supposedly a "pillar" among the apostles.[48] Or the challenge may arise from outside the community as the gospel is preached in a marketplace where Epicureans, Stoics, and many others promote their conflicting accounts of the nature of things, competing not only with the proclamation of Jesus and his resurrection but also with one another. The conflict is ever present. It may take the benign form of mutually respectful dialogue, but on occasion it becomes deadly.

In situations of perceived crisis, the truth of the gospel may need to be *confessed*. A formal confession is addressed to the church of its own day, but it is not intended to be merely ephemeral. As a solemn restatement of the truth of the gospel in the face of falsehood and injustice, it is also meant to be heard in the quite different

47. Acts 17:17–18.
48. Cf. Gal. 2:4, 9, 13–14.

circumstances that the future may bring. The Barmen Declaration is a relatively recent confession of this kind, and—for all its limitations—it remains instructive.

In May 1934, representatives of the German Lutheran, Reformed, and United Churches gathered in the industrial town of Barmen—part of the larger conurbation of Wuppertal—to reassert the church's independence of state control and to oppose the attempts of the so-called German Christians to bring it into line with Nazi ideology.[49] The Declaration was drafted primarily by Karl Barth, and its eloquent first article is as follows:

> Jesus Christ, as he is attested to us in Holy Scripture, is the one Word of God which we are to hear and which we are to trust and obey in life and in death.

> *Jesus Christus, wie er uns in der Heiligen Schrift bezeugt wird, ist das eine Wort Gottes, das wir zu hören, dem wir im Leben und im Sterben zu vertrauen und zu gehorchen haben.*[50]

To this positive assertion a negative corollary was added, rejecting the German Christian view that the divine word and will for the present were embodied in the pseudomessianic figure of the Führer. The article is prefaced by passages from the Gospel of John that provide a scriptural basis for both its positive and its negative assertions:

> Jesus Christ says: I am the Way and the Truth and the Life. No-one comes to the Father but through me (John 14:6).

> Truly, truly, I say to you: Whoever does not enter the sheepfold by the door, but climbs in another way, is a thief and a robber. . . . I am the Door. If anyone enters through me, he will be blessed (John 10:1, 9).

---

49. For the ecclesial-political context, see K. Scholder, *Churches and the Third Reich*, 2:122–71.

50. This statement remained exactly as Barth first drafted it, as did the second of the two Johannine passages that preceded it (John 10:1, 9). The first (John 14:6) appears to have been added later. See K. Scholder, *Churches and the Third Reich*, 2:138.

The truth of the gospel is here identified with Jesus Christ, who is himself the truth. The truth is assailed by falsehood, but Christ's word and promise still stand firm. The Declaration and its scriptural citations interpret current controversy about the shape and direction of the church in starkly antithetical terms that leave no room for confusion or compromise.

The subject of the article is "Jesus Christ, as he is attested to us in Holy Scripture." The name "Jesus Christ" occurs at or near the beginning of three of the four gospels, but only once later on. This name in this form is the foundation on which the Matthean, Markan, and Johannine narratives are constructed. Matthew opens with the words "The book of the genealogy of *Jesus Christ*" and proceeds to tell how "the birth of *Jesus Christ* was like this. . . ."[51] Mark announces "the beginning of the gospel of *Jesus Christ*," and John states that "grace and truth came through *Jesus Christ*."[52] The Barmen article does not confine Scripture's attestation of Jesus Christ to the gospels, but it follows them in naming him in this way and in naming him first. A specifically Johannine link is asserted not only in the passages cited but also in the allusion to the "Word." Jesus Christ is the one Word that we must hear: the Johannine *Logos* is understood as an audible word from God.[53] While the Word made flesh is seen and not heard in the Johannine prologue, the gospel refers elsewhere to the life-giving word spoken by Jesus that must be *heard* and believed.[54]

Jesus Christ as attested in Holy Scripture refers us to Jesus of Nazareth as he was received in the community he founded. While relative distinctions between the historical figure and his early reception may sometimes have their value, the construction of a "Jesus of history" who may be played off against a "Christ of faith" is problematic on both theological and historical grounds. Reconstructions of the historical Jesus tend to serve contemporary agendas. In one

51. Matt. 1:1, 18.
52. Mark 1:1; John 1:17. Elsewhere in the gospels "Jesus Christ" occurs only in John 17:3.
53. Cf. R. Bultmann, *Das Evangelium des Johannes*, 17–19 (Eng. trans., 34–36).
54. Cf. John 5:24, 25, 28; 10:27.

highly regarded work of the 1930s, Jesus' preaching of the kingdom of God reflects an "Aryan" strand in his cultural heritage rather than the "Israelite and Jewish" one.[55] In contrast, the Jesus Christ of the fourfold gospel is "the son of David, the son of Abraham."[56] The gospel rules out a non-Jewish Jesus. Neither is it a credible source for a Jesus accommodated to the current demand for a spirituality without church, scripture, or doctrine. Such a figure would not be the one Word of God of whom the gospel speaks.

The Jesus of the gospel is "the one Word of God which we are to hear and which we are to trust and obey in life and in death." The gospels tell the story of a particular human life and its outcome, yet that life may be understood as an act of communication so final and comprehensive that the whole span of our own lives is drawn into the sphere of this singular divine address. In this Word we live and move and have our being. This Word is the one Word *of God*. Although Jesus' presence dominates every page of all four gospels, it is also emphasized that he has come from God or is sent by God, and that in his words and works it is God who speaks to us and acts on our behalf. Jesus' presence is at the same time God's presence. God is no less present in the words and actions narrated in the gospels than is Jesus himself. That this is so is already clear from the additional name reserved for Jesus long before his birth: Emmanuel, God with us.

55. R. Otto, *Kingdom of God*, 13–44.
56. Matt. 1:1.

Bibliography

Where original-language editions of primary sources are listed, translations are my own. English translations are listed for information. In cases where footnote references have focused on modern editorial matter rather than the text, these are listed under "Secondary Sources."

Primary Sources

Apostolic Fathers. Edited by Bart D. Ehrman. 2 vols. LCL. Cambridge, MA: Harvard University Press, 2003.

The Apostolic Fathers—Justin Martyr—Irenaeus. ANF 1. Grand Rapids: Eerdmans, 1975.

Augustine. *De Consensu Evangelistarum*. Edited by F. Weihrich. CSEL 43. Vienna: Österreichische Akademie der Wissenschaften, 1904.

———. *Harmony of the Evangelists*. NPNF[1], vol. 6. Grand Rapids: Eerdmans, 1991.

Bede. *The Ecclesiastical History of the English Nation*. London: J. M. Dent; New York: E. P. Dutton, 1910.

Chrysostom, John. *Homilies on Matthew*. NPNF[1], vol. 10. Grand Rapids: Eerdmans, 1991.

Codex Fuldensis. Edited by E. Ranke. Marburg and Leipzig: N. G. Elwert, 1868.

Ephrem. *Saint Éphrem, Commentaire de l'Évangile concordant, texte syriaque*. Edited by L. Leloir. Dublin: Hoddaes Figgis, 1963.

———. *Saint Éphrem, Commentaire de l'Évangile concordant, version arménienne*. Edited by L. Leloir. Louvain: Peeters, 1953–54.

———. *Saint Ephrem's Commentary on Tatian's Diatessaron*. Translated by Carmel McCarthy. Oxford: Oxford University Press, 2000.

Eusebius. *Church History*. NPNF², vol. 1. Grand Rapids: Eerdmans, 1982.

———. *Eusebius Werke, Die Kirchengeschichte*. Edited by E. Schwartz and Theodor Mommsen. 3 vols. GCS. Leipzig: J. C. Hinrichs, 1903–9.

Evangelion da-Mepharreshe: The Curetonian Version of the Four Gospels, with the Readings of the Sinai Palimpsest and the Early Syriac Patristic Evidence. Edited by F. C. Burkitt. 2 vols. Cambridge: Cambridge University Press, 1904.

Irenaeus. *Libri Quinque Adversus Haereses*. Edited by W. W. Harvey. 2 vols. Cambridge: Cambridge University Press, 1857.

Jerome. *Commentarii in epistulam Pauli apostoli ad Galatas*. Edited by F. Bucchi. CCSL 77A. Turnhout: Brepols, 2006.

———. *Commentariorum in Matheum libri IV*. Edited by D. Hurst and M. Adriaen. CCSL 77. Turnhout: Brepols, 1969.

Josephus. *Jewish Antiquities*. Edited by H. St. J. Thackeray. 7 vols. LCL. Cambridge, MA: Harvard University Press; London: Heinemann, 1978–81.

———. *The Jewish War*. Edited by H. St. J. Thackeray. 2 vols. LCL. Cambridge, MA: Harvard University Press; London: Heinemann, 1976–79.

Justin Martyr. *Apologiae pro Christianis, Dialogus cum Tryphone*. Edited by M. Marcovich. New York: de Gruyter, 2005.

Lucretius. *On the Nature of Things*. Edited by W. H. D. Rouse and Martin F. Smith. LCL. Cambridge, MA: Harvard University Press, 1989.

Luther, Martin. *D. Martin Luthers Werke: Kritische Gesamtausgabe* (= WA, 121 vols.). Weimar: Hermann Böhlaus Nachfolger, 1883–2009.

———. *Luther's Works*. Edited by Jaroslav Pelikan and Helmut T. Lehmann. 55 vols. St. Louis: Concordia; Minneapolis: Fortress, 1957–86.

Origen. *Against Celsus*. ANF 4. Grand Rapids: Eerdmans, 1976.

———. *Commentary on Matthew*. ANF 10. Grand Rapids: Eerdmans, 1974.

———. *Commentary on the Gospel of John*. ANF 10. Grand Rapids: Eerdmans, 1974.

———. *Commentary on the Gospel according to John*. Edited by Ronald E. Heine. 2 vols. Washington, DC: Catholic University of America Press, 1989–93.

———. *Der Johanneskommentar*. Edited by E. Preuschen. GCS. Leipzig: J. C. Hinrichs, 1903.

———. *Homilien zu Lukas in der Übersetzung des Hieronymus und die griechischen Reste der Homilien und des Lukas-Kommentars*. Edited by Max Rauer. 2nd ed. GCS. Berlin: Akademie-Verlag, 1959.

———. *Homilies on Luke*. Translated by Joseph T. Lienhard, SJ. FC 94. Washington, DC: Catholic University of America Press, 1996.

———. *Origenes Werke, Erster Band: Die Schrift vom Martyrium, Buch I–IV Gegen Celsus*. Edited by P. Koetschau. GCS. Leipzig: J. C. Hinrichs, 1899.

Priscillian. *Priscillian of Avila: The Complete Works*. Edited by Marco Conti. Oxford: Oxford University Press, 2010.

Synopsis Quattuor Evangeliorum. Edited by K. Aland. 4th ed. Stuttgart: Württembergische Bibelanstalt, 1967.

Tatian. *Diatessaron*. ANF 10. Grand Rapids: Eerdmans, 1974.

————. *Diatessaron de Tatien*. Edited by A.-S. Marmardji. Beyrouth: Imprimerie Catholique, 1935.

Victorinus of Pettau. *Victorini Episcopi Petavionensis Opera*. Edited by J. Haussleiter. CSEL 49. Vienna: F. Tempsky; Leipzig: G. Freytag, 1916.

Secondary Sources

Alexander, J. J. G. *Insular Manuscripts, 6th to the 9th Century*. London: Harvey-Miller, 1978.

Barth, Karl. *Church Dogmatics*. Edited by G. W. Bromiley and T. F. Torrance. 14 vols. Edinburgh: T&T Clark, 1936–77.

Bauckham, Richard. *Jesus and the Eyewitnesses: The Gospels as Eyewitness Testimony*. Grand Rapids: Eerdmans, 2006.

Bausi, Alessandro. "The 'True Story' of the Abba Gärima Gospels." *Comparative Oriental Manuscript Studies Newsletter* 1 (January 2011): 17–20.

Bockmuehl, Markus. *Seeing the Word: Refocusing New Testament Study*. Grand Rapids: Baker Academic, 2006.

Brown, Michelle P. *The Lindisfarne Gospels and the Early Medieval World*. London: British Library, 2011.

Brown, Raymond E. *The Birth of the Messiah: A Commentary on the Infancy Narratives in the Gospels of Matthew and Luke*. 2nd ed. New York: Doubleday, 1993.

Bultmann, Rudolf. *Das Evangelium des Johannes*. 10th ed. KEK. Göttingen: Vandenhoeck & Ruprecht, 1968. Translated by G. R. Beasley-Murray, R. W. N. Hoare, and J. K. Riches as *The Gospel of John: A Commentary* (Oxford: Blackwell, 1971).

————. *Theology of the New Testament*. Translated by Kendrick Grobel. 2 vols. London: SCM, 1952–55. Originally published as *Theologie des Neuen Testaments* (Tübingen: Mohr, 1951).

Burridge, Richard A. *Imitating Jesus: An Inclusive Approach to New Testament Ethics*. Grand Rapids: Eerdmans, 2007.

———. *What Are the Gospels? A Comparison with Graeco-Roman Biography*. Grand Rapids: Eerdmans, 2004.

Childs, Brevard S. *The New Testament as Canon: An Introduction*. London: SCM, 1984.

Crawford, Matthew R. "Ammonius of Alexandria, Eusebius of Caesarea, and the Beginnings of Gospel Scholarship." *NTS* 61 (2015): 1–29.

———. "Diatessaron, a Misnomer? The Evidence of Ephrem's Commentary." *Early Christianity* 3 (2013): 362–85.

Davies, W. D., and D. C. Allison. *A Critical and Exegetical Commentary on the Gospel according to St. Matthew*. 3 vols. ICC. Edinburgh: T&T Clark, 1988–97.

Gameson, Richard. *From Holy Island to Durham: The Context and Meanings of the Lindisfarne Gospels*. London: Third Millennium, 2013.

Gathercole, Simon J. *Defending Substitution: An Essay on Atonement in Paul*. Grand Rapids: Baker Academic, 2015.

———. *The Gospel of Thomas: Introduction and Commentary*. Leiden: Brill, 2014.

———. "The Titles of the Gospels in the Earliest New Testament Manuscripts." *ZNW* 104 (2013): 33–76.

Goodacre, Mark. *The Case against Q: Studies in Markan Priority and the Synoptic Problem*. Harrisburg, PA: Trinity Press International, 2002.

Grafton, Anthony, and Megan Williams. *Christianity and the Transformation of the Book*. Cambridge, MA: Harvard University Press, 2006.

Hays, Richard B. *Reading Backwards: Figural Christology and the Fourfold Gospel Witness*. Waco: Baylor University Press, 2014.

Hengel, Martin. *The Four Gospels and the One Gospel of Jesus Christ.* Translated by John Bowden. London: SCM, 2000.

Hurtado, Larry W. *The Earliest Christian Artifacts: Manuscripts and Christian Origins.* Grand Rapids: Eerdmans, 2006.

Kraus, Thomas J., Michael J. Kruger, and Tobias Nicklas, eds. *Gospel Fragments.* Oxford: Oxford University Press, 2009.

Kraus, Thomas J., and Tobias Nicklas, eds. *Das Petrusevangelium und die Petrusapokalypse: Die griechischen Fragmente mit deutscher und englischer Übersetzung.* GCS. Berlin: de Gruyter, 2004.

Leroy, Jules. "Un nouvel évangéliaire éthiopien illustré du monastère d'Abba Garima." In *Synthronon: Art et archéologie de la fin de l'antiquité et du moyen âge,* edited by A. Grabar et al., 75–87. Paris: Librairie C. Klincksieck, 1968.

McGurk, Patrick. *Latin Gospel Books from A.D. 400 to A.D. 800.* Paris-Brussels: Aux Éditions "Érasme"; Anvers-Amsterdam: Standaard-Boekhandel, 1961.

McKenzie, Judith, and Francis Watson. *Early Illuminated Gospel Books from Ethiopia.* Oxford: Manar al-Athar; Amsterdam: Allard Pierson Museum (forthcoming).

Metzger, Bruce M. *A Textual Commentary on the Greek New Testament.* New York: United Bible Societies, 1975.

Mitchell, Margaret. "Patristic Counter-Evidence to the Claim That 'The Gospels Were Written for All Christians.'" *NTS* 51 (2005): 36–79.

Nestle, Eberhard. "Die Eusebianische Evangelien-Synopse." *NKZ* 19 (1908): 40–51, 93–114, 219–32.

Nordenfalk, Carl. *Die spätantiken Kanontafeln: Kunstgeschichtliche Studien über die eusebianische Evangelien-Konkordanz in den vier ersten Jahrhunderten ihrer Geschichte.* Göteborg: O. Isacson, 1938.

Otto, Rudolf. *The Kingdom of God and the Son of Man: A Study in the History of Religion.* Translated by Floyd V. Filson and Bertram Lee Woolf. London: Lutterworth, 1943.

Scholder, Klaus. *The Churches and the Third Reich*. 2 vols. London: SCM, 1987–88.

Soden, Hermann von. *Die Schriften des Neuen Testaments in ihrer ältesten erreichbaren Textgestalt hergestellt auf Grund ihrer Textgeschichte*, I.1. Berlin: Duncker, 1902.

Steinmetz, David. "The Superiority of Pre-Critical Exegesis." *ThTo* 37 (1980): 27–38.

Swanson, Reuben J., ed. *New Testament Greek Manuscripts: Variant Readings Arranged in Horizontal Lines against Codex Vaticanus—Luke*. Sheffield: Sheffield Academic Press; Pasadena, CA: William Carey International University Press, 1995.

Trobisch, David. *The First Edition of the New Testament*. Oxford: Oxford University Press, 2000.

Tuckett, Christopher. *The Gospel of Mary*. Oxford: Oxford University Press, 2007.

Wallraff, Martin. *Kodex und Kanon: Das Buch im frühen Christentum*. Berlin: de Gruyter, 2013.

Watson, Francis. "Bultmann and the Theological Interpretation of Scripture." In *Beyond Bultmann: Reckoning a New Testament Theology*, edited by Bruce W. Longenecker and Mikeal C. Parsons, 257–72, 320–24. Waco: Baylor University Press, 2014.

———. *Gospel Writing: A Canonical Perspective*. Grand Rapids: Eerdmans, 2013.

———. "Towards a Redaction-Critical Reading of the Diatessaron Gospel" (forthcoming).

Webster, John. *Holy Scripture: A Dogmatic Sketch*. Cambridge: Cambridge University Press, 2003.

Wormald, Francis. *The Miniatures in the Gospel of St Augustine (Corpus Christi College Ms. 286)*. Cambridge: Cambridge University Press, 1954.

Index of Subjects

Index of Authors

Index of Scripture
and Other Ancient Sources